Worship, Mission, and the Church Year

Worship, Mission, and the Church Year

How Union with Christ Forms
Worshipers for Mission in Every Season

NICHOLAS W. MONSMA

CASCADE *Books* • Eugene, Oregon

WORSHIP, MISSION, AND THE CHURCH YEAR
How Union with Christ Forms Worshipers for Mission in Every Season

Copyright © 2019 Nicholas W. Monsma. All rights reserved. Except for brief quotations in critical publications or reviews, no part of this book may be reproduced in any manner without prior written permission from the publisher. Write: Permissions, Wipf and Stock Publishers, 199 W. 8th Ave., Suite 3, Eugene, OR 97401.

Cascade Books
An Imprint of Wipf and Stock Publishers
199 W. 8th Ave., Suite 3
Eugene, OR 97401

www.wipfandstock.com

PAPERBACK ISBN: 978-1-5326-1869-7
HARDCOVER ISBN: 978-1-4982-8607-7
EBOOK ISBN: 978-1-4982-4447-3

Cataloguing-in-Publication data:

Names: Monsma, Nicholas W., author.
Title: Worship, mission, and the church year : how union with Christ forms worshipers for mission in every season / Nicholas W. Monsma.
Description: Eugene, OR: Cascade Books, 2019 | Includes bibliographical references and index.
Identifiers: ISBN 978-1-5326-1869-7 (paperback) | ISBN 978-1-4982-8607-7 (hardcover) | ISBN 978-1-4982-4447-3 (ebook)
Subjects: LCSH: Church year | Missions—Theory | Liturgics | Mission of the church
Classification: BV30 M657 2019 (print) | BV30 (ebook)

Manufactured in the U.S.A.   FEBRUARY 5, 2019

Scriptures taken from the Holy Bible, New International Version®, NIV®. Copyright © 1973, 1978, 1984, 2011 by Biblica, Inc.™ Used by permission of Zondervan. All rights reserved worldwide. www.zondervan.com The "NIV" and "New International Version" are trademarks registered in the United States Patent and Trademark Office by Biblica, Inc.™

Table of Contents

Acknowledgments vii

Introduction: Worship as Missional Formation, Participation, and Union with Christ 1

1. The Birth of Jesus 20
2. The Peripatetic Ministry of Jesus 33
3. The Suffering, Crucifixion, and Death of Jesus 52
4. The Resurrection of Jesus 74
5. The Ascension of Jesus 95
6. The Return of Jesus 112

Epilogue 133

Bibliography 135
Name/Subject Index 139
Scripture Index 143

Acknowledgments

God has blessed me by putting a number of people in my life without whom I could not have started work on, much less completed, this book. I thank God for my mother, Leda Monsma, and my mother-in-law, Jere Meade, who each lived at my home to care for my children during the periods when I left for Gordon-Conwell Theological Seminary to study many of the ideas at the heart of this book. I thank God for Paul Detterman and Jim Singleton, my professors, mentors, and friends, who explored the concepts of mission and worship with me during the three years of my DMin studies. I also am grateful for their suggestion that I go on to explore the specific topic of this book: missional worship and its relationship to the liturgical calendar.

I'm thankful for the patience and love of the worshipers at East Palmyra Christian Reformed Church who worship God with me each Sunday, and who keep me constantly aware of the reality that worship is not first of all something to be examined in books but something to be practiced by real people in a real church, with all its struggles and joys.

I'm grateful for the help of the Calvin Institute of Christian Worship, specifically for John Witvliet, who encouraged me to seek a publisher for this work, and for Noel Snyder, who devoted time to reviewing a draft of this book and providing invaluable feedback that helped to steer it in the right direction.

I'm grateful for the proofreading done by my lovely sister Rebecca DenHollander (who suggested that I call her "lovely" here). I'm especially grateful for my lovely wife Kelly Monsma (whom I'm calling "lovely" of my own volition). Yes, she patiently listened (or at least convincingly pretended to listen) as I excitedly talked about all the ideas in this book, and she reviewed a manuscript. But mostly, I'm grateful that she eagerly partners with

Acknowledgments

me to answer all of the calls we hear from God—not just the call to work on this project, but at the same time, to raise our children, to serve our community, to love each other, and much more.

To God alone be the glory!

Introduction

*Worship as Missional Formation,
Participation, and Union with Christ*

"Talk about Jesus more." That's the advice I've given to people as they struggle to discuss their Christian faith with inquisitive friends. I don't mean that they should talk about church. I don't mean that they should talk about the Bible. I don't mean that they should talk about prayer. I don't even mean that they should simply talk about God. I mean that they should talk about Jesus himself, God the Son, the person who took on human flesh, who took on our human suffering and our human guilt, who died, who rose, who ascended, who sent his Holy Spirit, and who will return. When someone asks us about our faith or why we go to church, it is easy for us to pull the plug and let all of the power of the gospel drain from the conversation. We talk about how great our church is, or we offer the vague hope that "God has a plan for our lives." When we don't talk specifically about Jesus, and about him by name, our church-going begins to sound like some kind of generic religious practice. Our faith starts to sound like some kind of generic belief in God. All of this changes, however, if we make a point of talking about Jesus Christ, specifically and by name. Talk about Jesus more, and your conversations will be oriented to the very heart of God's mission.

It's wisdom that many preachers have learned: "Preach about Jesus more." Something is different when we start talking about Jesus Christ. Recently, I experienced this difference as I neared the end of a sermon. I read the words Jesus used to summon his disciples in the Garden of Gethsemane: "Rise, let us go! Here comes my betrayer!" (Matt 26:46). I took a minute or two to reflect on this profound willingness of Jesus. He was willing to sacrifice his own life for the salvation of the world. During those last few minutes, I turned the topic of the sermon to Jesus himself and his saving work. Something changed in the room—or at least it felt like it to me. I sensed that we in the room were being oriented to the heart of God's mission. Something is different when we start talking about the saving life and work of Jesus Christ, when we preach about Jesus more.

This is also good advice for worship: "Worship about Jesus more." That is what this book is about. Worship that is about Jesus goes beyond merely speaking his name in prayer or song. When worship is about Jesus, the liturgy leads us toward union with Jesus Christ. When worship is about Jesus, we are formed and transformed by that union with him. When worship is about Jesus, we are changed. When we worship about Jesus more, our whole lives are oriented to the heart of God's mission.

This book examines what it means to be formed for our God-given mission by worshiping "about Jesus" throughout the seasons of the church year. The church calendar marks key events in the life and work of Jesus—from his birth at Christmas, through his suffering on Good Friday, all the way to his return during Advent. Following that calendar gives us opportunities for our worship to be "about Jesus" and for us to be formed through union with Christ for our God-given mission in seasonally changing ways. By saying all this, we assume three things:

- That worship should form us for our mission,
- That worshipers should be participants in worship, and
- That worship is union with Christ.

Let's examine those three assumptions.

Worship Should Form Us for Mission

We can take the assumption that worship should form us for mission too far. Pastor and theologian Christopher J. Schoon warns about the "assembly-line view of worship,"[1] in which we expect that good worship will take worshipers in, do something to them, and spit out people who act in a different way. Theologian Simon Chan also identifies this as a problem and explains that when the church gathers for worship, we shouldn't do this to

---

1. Schoon, "Communally Embodied Gospel," 139–41.

Introduction

accomplish some other goal. The church should gather for worship *in order to worship*. Worship is not a means to an end, that is, a tool to accomplish something else. "The end of worship is worship."[2] In fact, worship (glorifying God and fully enjoying him forever) is "the chief and highest end of man," to use the language of the Westminster catechisms.[3] The purpose, the goal, the hoped-for outcome of engaging in worship ought to be simply that God is worshiped.

Worship should be about worship. We should treat the worship of the one, true God as an end in itself. Even so, many of us have a hard time resisting the urge to treat worship as a means to an end—especially when we are passionate about the mission of the church. This is common in congregations that have an attractional ministry mindset in which church leadership "engineer[s] the church 'product' to attract their preferred clientele."[4] The worship wars of previous decades were often fought by people treating worship as a means to an end. One side seemed to agitate for any change that would make worship more relevant or responsive to felt-needs or more effective at attracting large numbers.[5] The other side—those who wanted to retain the congregation's traditional forms of worship—also seemed to treat worship as a means to an end. I've personally been told by some who care deeply about the growth of the church that worship must include classic hymns and organ accompaniment because that's what is familiar to their friends and relatives who have strayed from the church. Don't we want worship to feel like that familiar thing they've been missing for so long? When one of our greatest hopes for our church building is that it would be filled with people, and our most common activity together is worship, it is hard not to turn worship into a tool for filling the pews.

Means-to-an-end thinking is common enough in congregations that are more "missional" too. These churches would prefer to think of the church's task as a matter of being sent out into the world with the gospel, and worship is a tempting means to this end. Some view weekly gathered worship as a reprieve from during-the-week missional work, during which the church is reenergized for that mission.[6] Worshipers escape from the grit and grime of their God-given mission in the world to get a taste of the

---

2. Chan, *Liturgical Theology*, 53.
3. "Larger Catechism," Q&A 1.
4. Frost, *The Road to Missional*, 21.
5. Chan, *Liturgical Theology*, 41.
6. Schattauer, "Liturgical Assembly," 2–3.

3

heavenly banquet and a glimpse of the heavenly glory. Worship leaders ask what will best fill these worshipers up so they can be sent out for the week ahead, and soon worship is treated as a means to an end. Other missional congregations view weekly gathered worship as a means of calling worshipers to engage in mission.[7] Some use the worship as a subtle, subconscious call to mission by modeling in worship the kind of missional engagement that the worshipers are expected to engage in during the week.[8] For example, "passing the peace" becomes practice for peacemaking with others during the week. The worship leaders might not say as much, but the practice is included for the sake of encouraging worshipers to continue to do that same thing at other times. Worship leaders check to see that the language used in songs, sermons, and prayers is contextualized with local, casual idioms. The hope is that as worshipers hear this language in worship, they will sense a call to speak about the gospel in a similar way with the people they meet on Tuesday and Wednesday. Worship leaders can be more explicit too. The call to mission doesn't have to be subconscious. At times, worshipers are directly encouraged to go out and get involved in a variety of missional activities.[9] The worshipers are told to go and tell others about the resurrection of Jesus. The worshipers are told to volunteer at the food pantry. Worship leaders ask themselves: how can we use worship to encourage worshipers, directly and indirectly, to get involved in mission? When our greatest hope for the church is that it would be sent out to engage in missional activity, it is tempting to turn worship into a tool for getting that done.

But is it always wrong to give in to this temptation to think of worship as a means to an end? Is there some sense in which worship is *both* an end in itself *and* a means to an end? Even those who argue that worship shouldn't be treated as a means to an end will insist at other times on treating worship that way nevertheless.[10] For example, theologian Ruth Meyers writes against using worship as an instrument for mission, but then she goes on to suggest some images for understanding the relationship between worship and mission that make it look like worship is being used as an instrument for mission.[11] Similarly, while pleading for the church and its

---

7. Meyers, *Missional Worship*, 33–34.
8. Witvliet, *Worship Seeking Understanding*, 106–7.
9. Meyers, *Missional Worship*, 31–34.
10. Schoon, "Communally Embodied Gospel," 137.
11. Meyers, *Missional Worship*, 34–45.

INTRODUCTION

worship to be understood as ends-in-themselves, Chan doesn't seem to object to all kinds of instrumental relationships between worship and the church's mission. He writes of how worship is formational and has a missiological orientation.[12]

It might seem so compelling to say that worship is an end in itself and not a means to an end, but the connection between worship and formation for mission is more complicated than that. Worship and mission aren't as distinct as we might think. One of the images Ruth Meyers suggests for understanding the relationship between worship and mission is a Möbius strip. A Möbius strip is a continuous belt with one twist in it. Because it has only one twist, it appears to have two sides, but it actually only has one. Try it. Go to your closet, take out an ordinary belt, and thread the end through the buckle upside down. Now run your finger along the belt, and by the time you get back to the exact place you started, you'll have run your finger on "both sides." How is that possible? With that one twist, your belt has become a Möbius strip and has only one side, even though it appears to have two. Worship and mission are related to each other just like the "sides" of a Möbius strip. Worship and mission, Meyers writes, might appear to be distinct activities, but they run into one another in such a way that it is impossible to find the dividing line between them. One becomes the other.[13] For this reason, even when we treat worship as an end in itself, we should expect that worship has the capacity for worship to strengthen mission. "Worship that is mission shapes a people for mission."[14]

Even if *we* treat worship as an end in itself, God the Holy Spirit might often use our worshiping as means to an end. There can be—and should be—a distinction between what *we* are doing in worship and what *God the Holy Spirit* is doing in worship. When we assemble for worship, our goal should be to worship. However, as we gather for the simple purpose of worshiping, God himself might be gathering us for other purposes, and perhaps he intends to form us for our mission. For this reason, worship leaders need to take a close look at the liturgy, the specific practices the congregation engages in during worship, like songs, prayers, preaching, sacraments, and so on, and the order in which they do these things. Ask: will your congregation's liturgies, that specific set of practices you have planned to lead worshipers through, place obstacles in the way of this formation?

12. Chan, *Liturgical Theology*, 21–60, especially 55, 78, 87.
13. Meyers, *Missional Worship*, 34–38.
14. Ibid., 37.

Will your liturgy turn them away from or toward the potential missional-formation work of the Holy Spirit? And importantly for the sake of this book: what might missionally-formative liturgies look like during each season of the church year?

Worshipers Should Participate in Worship

The next assumption seems obvious: of course worshipers should participate in worship. Even so, we often fail to live up to this. Sure, worshipers *should* be active participants, but many of us have learned the habit of acting like an audience of passive observers, even consumers. We assume the posture of an audience, we observe and evaluate rather than participate. But worship is fundamentally different from a lecture, or a concert, or a play. In worship, the leaders are not performers, and the rest are not a mere audience. Together, we should all be participants. *All* should be singing in praise, not just the vocalists; *all* should praying, not just the worship leader; *all* should be meditating on God's word to hear the Spirit's message of grace, not just the preacher; *all* should be worshiping together according to the liturgy. But we are far too happy to observe as the worship leaders and a few super-spiritual neighbors do the actual participation. When we assume the posture of an audience, and when we begin to observe and evaluate rather than participate, we resist the Holy Spirit's work.

This is why I find it hard to respond when people say, "Good sermon!" At times I have simply said, "Thank you." Worshipers say these things to me as we shake hands on the way out of the worship space. There's often not a lot of time for conversation. It's easiest for me to accept their words for what they were—expressions of gratitude—and respond in the typical way: "Thank you." But then my heart sinks because I have reinforced a misconception about worship: that worship is a product offered by worship leaders for the consumption and satisfaction of the worshipers. A compliment for a good sermon is most appropriate when a person was observing and evaluating, a member of an audience. But that's not what (I hope) is happening in worship. I'm not offering a product for the audience to assess. I'm opening up the word of God so we can all hear him speak. I should say, "Praise God," instead of "Thank you." My heart sinks deeper when I realize that even I think of worship like this at times. In my own church, even though I eschew being praised for my leadership in worship, I also know that I crave that praise. When I am in other churches, even though I say that I look forward to joining in and participating in the worship, I find that I observe and evaluate far too much of the time. I too act like worshipers are observers and worship leaders are producers and performers. However, I and others should be participants together in worship, and if we were, the fruit of that participation would be Christian formation—specifically formation for mission by the Holy Spirit.

This formation happens because regular, ritualized practices like the liturgies we use in worship shape our habits. Christian philosopher James K. A. Smith has written extensively on this. Human beings, Smith argues, do what they do less as a result of deliberation and decision and more as a result of habit. Human action is less a matter of the intellect and more a matter of the heart.[15] When I walk over to my church's building, I usually find that when I get there I have the church keys in my pocket. Why? Not always because I think to myself, before I leave the house, "I'd better grab the church keys before I go." Often, I don't think about grabbing the keys at all. I grab them because I am in the habit of doing so. (I'm sure I learned the habit after repeatedly arriving at church without the keys!) I have even found the church keys in my pocket on walks when I wasn't heading to church. We learn habits like this through repetition, and the liturgies we use in worship are the kinds of repetitions that can form our Christian habits: "Our identity and love are shaped 'liturgically' precisely because liturgies are those rituals and practices that constitute the embodied stories of a body politic."[16] Pay close attention to those three important concepts: "embodied," "stories," and "body politic." They represent three reasons that human beings are creatures of habits: we have bodies, we tell ourselves stories, and we live in relationships with others.

Embodied

We have bodies that relate to the world in specific ways, and this is why we find ourselves with some habits and not others.[17] Compare, for example, how the thoughts and habits of someone who is less than five feet tall differ from those of someone who is taller than six feet. Each of them sees the world, imagines their body in the world, and relates to the world in different ways. It's not that they decide to relate to the world in different

---

15. Smith, *Imagining the Kingdom*, 31.
16. Ibid., 109.
17. Ibid., 31–41.

ways. Rather, because they live in the world in their unique bodies, they find themselves with different thoughts and habits.

This is one of the reasons that participation in worship has the power to form us. When we participate in worship, we participate with our bodies. Worship is "designed to engage us both mentally and by way of our senses, with each reinforcing the other."[18] Music is a great example of this participation. Music is easily participatory, non-directional, and accompanies. In other words, music can surround worshipers, and music can support the meaning of the accompanying words.[19] Theologian Clayton Schmit specifically recommends folk music because it is created with the capacities of the ordinary, untrained person in mind. Folk music encourages participation.[20] Similar things could surely be said for other kinds of art—rhetoric, architecture, and functional sculpture, for example. Art forms best suited for worship are those that encourage bodily participation and thereby facilitate the formation of the worshipers' habits. We enter worship and hear a call to worship, and our bodies learn the habit of being part of a people who owe their existence to God's election and call. We close our eyes, bow our heads, and quiet ourselves in a prayer of confession. As we do, our bodies learn the habit of quiet humility before God. We sit and listen to a sermon and stand to respond with a profession of faith. Our bodies learn to be people of the word—of the good news and of the response of faith. We eat and drink from the table, and our bodies learn that we depend not on something we bring out from within, but upon what God brings into us from outside. Our habits are shaped because worship involves our bodies.

Stories

Human beings rely on the stories told in our imaginations. Our imaginations contribute to our way of being in the world in a major way, and our imaginations depend on language, especially metaphors. We prefer certain metaphors to others, and together our collection of metaphors results in a certain story.[21] We tell ourselves this story about the way things are. This primes us to continue to experience things according to that story. Things feel right to us when they fit the narrative.

18. Benson, *Liturgy*, 135.
19. Schmit, *Sent and Gathered*, 104.
20. Ibid., 98–99.
21. Smith, *Imagining the Kingdom*, 110–37.

INTRODUCTION

Worship shapes our habits because when we participate in the liturgy, we are brought into a story. "Liturgies are formative because—and just to the extent that—they tap into our imaginative core."[22] If liturgy is about narrative, participants in that liturgy slowly learn that narrative as their own. Pastor Mike Cosper describes how liturgy can teach worshipers the story of the gospel—creation, fall, redemption, and consummation.[23] Of course, the story can be taught to worshipers in big, obvious ways. The pastor or worship leader can tell the story outright, and this can surely form us for mission. If we wonder how worship can help form us for mission in union with Christ during Christmas, for example, the most obvious way is for the pastor to preach on the Christmas-related dimensions of missional union with Christ. If we want the worshipers to learn the story of the gospel, we can simply tell it. I've done that. It's obvious. Everyone who is paying attention to the sermon gets the message.

In this book, however, we're going to look at more subtle worship practices. There are a number of reasons for this. First off, telling the story outright in sermons is too obvious. Of course preaching is one of the ways to bring these themes of missional union with Christ into worship and have worshipers formed by them. If you are a preacher, I encourage you to do that. But we need more ideas than that. Worship is much more than a sermon, so we should think about what *else* we can do. How can other parts of the liturgy tell that story? And sure, the preacher could keep hammering away at one particular theme throughout a whole season of preaching, but if that theme is so significant, it should keep showing up in smaller ways, throughout the liturgy, even when the sermons are addressing other themes. You can sit down and eat a whole pile of turkey breast on Thanksgiving Day, but what are you going to do with the leftovers after that? You'll want to think about ways to include that turkey in sandwiches and casseroles for other meals. After preaching on the themes of missional union with Christ, a church will want to find ways for these themes to be included in worship on other Sundays. That's what the rest of this book focuses on.

But that leads to a second reason to focus on these more subtle ways to include these themes in liturgy: it might be more formative to have these themes in the background than in the foreground. One of my mentors spoke about his experience: the longer a pastor is with a congregation, the more the congregation begins to be like that pastor. (It's a scary thought for any

---

22. Smith, *Imagining the Kingdom*, 137.
23. Cosper, *Rhythms of Grace*, 117–50.

pastor! Do I really want my fellow churchgoers to become more like me!?) How does something like this happen? Probably not because pastors tell congregations who they are and instruct the congregations to become more like them. Rather, over the course of years, whenever the pastor prayers, or talks with church members, or leads meetings, or introduces songs to sing, or gives special announcements, or serves at a potluck, or plays with the children, or whatever, that pastor's personality shows. Everything the pastor does happens against the background of that pastor's personality, and the congregation learns that personality.

The same is true in worship. Worshipers are formed by a story when the pastor preaches that gospel story. But worshipers will be formed by the themes of that story just as much, if not more, when those themes form the background of worship, when they are there all the time in subtle ways. This is because the motions of worship itself lead worshipers through a narrative, and as participants in the liturgy, worshipers begin to learn that narrative for themselves. When worshipers begin by singing songs and praying prayers of adoration, they absorb a narrative that begins with a holy God who created the world. When worshipers continue with a prayer of confession and words from God that assure them they are forgiven, they absorb a narrative whose central conflict involves human rebellion and the need to be reconciled with God. They absorb a narrative whose hero is Jesus Christ, giving himself for the salvation of the world. When worshipers conclude worship with the Lord's Supper and a God who blesses them as he sends them out into the world, they absorb a narrative that is about active hope.

Worshipers absorb the narrative even from the tiniest bits of speech. Repeating the smallest bits of speech can encourage a worshiper's imagination to begin preferring certain metaphors to others. Christian worship is filled with words—in prayers, preaching, verbal guidance, professions of faith, and such like. Worship has transformative power, Smith writes, partly because the words used have the power to form the basic orientational metaphors that shape a worshiper's conceptual map.[24] Words are used to instruct, but they are also used to guide believers in expressing their faith. Words are used aesthetically to fit the believer's situation—their place in the story, their orientation to the world and its redemption in Christ. Words are used to carry into the present the memories of the saints who have gone before. When worshipers participate in a liturgy which immerses them in

---

24. Smith, *Imagining the Kingdom*, 110–24. See also Rienstra and Rienstra, *Worship Words*.

a story, that story slowly becomes their own. That is a second reason that worship has the capacity to form the habits of the worshipers.

Body Politic

Human beings are social creatures. Each of us relates to the world in a specific way because we have learned this way of relating from our social environment. Within a community, each generation is given a set of traditions from those who went before. These traditions end up embedded in institutions. We don't really belong to a community or an institution (like a church) until we have learned the traditions.[25] Our habits as human beings are received from and reinforced by our communities and their institutions.

This is another reason that worship has the power to form our habits. Worship itself is an essentially *social* exercise. We worship in community and under the influence of institutions. This connection between worship and community is found in many of the classic worship-related texts in the New Testament. For example, John tells us that Jesus spoke about worship with a Samaritan woman: "God is spirit, and his worshipers must worship in the Spirit and in truth" (John 4:24). This short conversation occurred in the midst of an episode that challenges assumptions about the social boundaries of the followers of Jesus. May Samaritans be part of this community too? Questions about true worship can't be answered except in the context of questions about true community. In the book of Acts, Luke tells us what the worship of the early church was like, and includes a striking description of close community:

> They devoted themselves to the apostles' teaching and to fellowship, to the breaking of bread and to prayer. Everyone was filled with awe at the many wonders and signs performed by the apostles. All the believers were together and had everything in common. They sold property and possessions to give to anyone who had need. (Acts 2:42–45)

In both Romans 12 and 1 Corinthians 10–13, Paul writes about worship and immediately follows that with discussions of the "body of Christ." Biblical worship is, first of all, a corporate activity.

Notice how the very act of gathering together with others for worship can form us through our social environment. Many of us find ourselves

---

25. Smith, *Imagining the Kingdom*, 81–84.

scattered from our church community during the rest of the week. Occasionally we see fellow church members, but we mostly interact with others outside the congregation. Then Sunday comes, and we gather for weekly worship. There's something formative about being with our little corner of the church again. We join the body, and we learn to be the church in a way that we couldn't if we weren't together in the same room. The social environment of worship is also reinforced during communal activities that draw upon unity and reconciliation, like singing, professing faith together with one voice, and praying for one another. Worship has a particular power to form worshipers because they are participants not just in a liturgy but in a *social* liturgy.

I learned this unexpectedly as I did my Doctor of Ministry research. As part of my thesis-project, I introduced some lay commissionings into the liturgy. During worship, I invited one member of the congregation forward to tell us what challenges and opportunities they would face in the coming week. Then we prayed for them, commissioning them to their mission in ordinary life. Afterward, I received feedback from a focus group. I anticipated that the focus group would report that they felt somehow equipped for their own part of God's mission as they witnessed these commissionings. They reported a little bit of this, but mostly they kept talking about how the commissionings made the congregation feel more like a unified body. I was a little disappointed. *I didn't introduce the commissionings just so you could get to know each other better*, I thought. *I did it so you could be equipped for your God-given mission.* I had hoped the commissioning liturgy would strengthen mission, but it seemed that it had a greater effect on strengthening community.

It occurs to me now that strengthening community might actually be part of strengthening mission. Alyssa feels more connected to Zach as he is commissioned for his ordinary missional opportunities. Through this, Alyssa learns the habits of mission herself—through that social environment. When we gather together as a body, participating in the liturgy, we learn missional habits from the community, just as we learn missional habits from the narrative that is told and from our bodily participation in the liturgy. Because true worship involves these aspects of habit-forming participation in the liturgy, worship has the power to form us for our mission.

INTRODUCTION

Worship Is Union with Christ

The third assumption is perhaps the most important: worship is union with Christ. That's why it is useful to think about missionally formative liturgy throughout the seasons of the church year. The seasons of the church year follow the life and work of Jesus Christ, and it is in union with Christ that we are formed for our mission. Worship is union with Christ, and our liturgical calendar takes us through the life and work of Jesus Christ season by season.

Theologian J. Todd Billings quotes New Testament scholar Richard Longenecker: "Being 'in Christ' is the essence of Christian proclamation and experience."[26] Theologian Lewis Smedes goes further: "Being in Christ is not only the fundamental fact of the individual Christian's experience, it is the whole new reality."[27] Union with Christ really is everything, and it can be explored in a number of ways.[28] In the New Testament, Paul writes of individuals being "in Christ," of this being true of a whole congregation collectively, of their life lived "in Christ," and of his own apostleship "in Christ."[29] It's such a compelling kernel of theology that it has spawned a hundred different interpretations: some see union with Christ as something accomplished primarily in the incarnation, others in the crucifixion, still others in the ascension and promised return of Christ;[30] some understand that we are in Christ as a matter of location, others as a matter of existence or being, and still others as a matter of our belonging or situation.[31]

Union with Christ is about everything we are called to be and do as the people of God. "The disciples were called Christians first at Antioch" (Acts 11:26). The word "Christian" only shows up a couple of other times in the New Testament, but it clearly became one of the most important words for the followers of Jesus. In the decades that followed, martyrs were sentenced to death after saying the words: "I am a Christian." We are Christians. We hold to Christian theology. We engage in Christian activities. We sing Christian songs. We support Christian institutions. We promote Christian

---

26. Richard Longenecker, quoted in Billings, *Union with Christ*, 1.
27. Smedes, *Union with Christ*, 59.
28. See Calvin, *Institutes*, 3.1.1; Smedes, *Union with Christ*; Billings, *Union with Christ*.
29. Smedes, *Union with Christ*, 55–57.
30. Ibid., 1–25.
31. Ibid., 58–67.

values. If we don't intentionally connect all these "Christian" things to the "Christ" whose name they bear, then "Christian" is just a label.

So, what does the word "Christian" mean? It sounds like a dumb question. It's obvious, isn't it? A Christian is someone who in some way follows or is associated with Christ, just like a Marxist is someone who follows Marx. But this is no dumb question. This question is significant enough to have a place among the 129 questions of the Heidelberg Catechism: "But why are you called a Christian?" To be a Christian is not just to follow Christ or be associated with Christ. To be a Christian is to "share in his anointing," says the answer.[32] To be a Christian is to have union with Christ; it is to belong to that new situation that he created. And if that's who we are, then every part of our lives as saved people is about Christ.

In union with Christ we receive all the blessings of salvation—both the blessings we receive passively as a gift, and those we receive actively through hard work.[33] Because union with Christ is such an expansive theme and at the foundation of Christian theology and experience, it is a platform from which we can dive into all the dimensions of Christian life and church ministry. Billings shows how a theology of union with Christ can help the church get through some of its current theological struggles in the West, struggles like a growing sense that God is a generic deity, the presumption that human beings are pretty good, a difficulty imaging God as holy and other, a liberal-conservative divide over social justice, and the difficulties with the idea of "incarnational ministry."[34]

Worship, too, is one of those realities of Christian life and church ministry that springs from union with Christ and that a theology of union with Christ can help explain. We offer our worship *"to the Father, through the Son, in the Holy Spirit,"* as the saying goes.[35] This is ultimately why worship can form us for our mission. It's not just because the Holy Spirit can use liturgy as a tool for this purpose. It's not just because we participate deeply in the liturgy. It is because worshipers are united to Jesus Christ in worship. Union with Christ results Christian formation: "we will grow to become in every respect the mature body of him who is the head, that is, Christ. From him the whole body, joined and held together by every supporting

---

32. "Heidelberg Catechism," Q&A 32.
33. Billings, *Calvin, Participation*, 106–8.
34. Billings, *Union with Christ*.
35. Parry, *Worshipping Trinity*, 71; Torrance, *Worship, Community*, 20; Chan, *Liturgical Theology*, 47.

INTRODUCTION

ligament, grows and builds itself up in love, as each part does its work" (Eph 4:15–16).

We don't always think about worship as a transforming union with Christ. Theologian James B. Torrance describes a God-and-me view of worship that is common across Christian traditions: As we arrive at the church building a few minutes before the first song, too often we imagine that we have come to worship to perform our religious service for God. We intend to offer him our modern-day sacrifices—our attention, our singing, our prayers, our financial gifts. We hope to go away from worship with a refreshed sense of who God is and what he has done. The work of Jesus Christ seems little more than that prior work which enables us to have this relationship with God in the here-and-now. Worship is about God and me.[36] In a similar way, Dutch theologian F. Gerrit Immink writes about how worship is internalized and personalized. Many of us are skeptical of any practices in worship that seem "magical"—that would seem to conjure the presence of God through human activity. As a result, we expect that whatever the spiritual aspect of worship is, it is something that is mostly inside our minds. As we devote our attention to God, we expect to "meet" him only inasmuch as we feel his presence internally, personally, and privately.[37] Worship is about God and me, we think, but that is not true Christian worship.

In true Christian worship, God is present in three persons. Worship is participation "through the Spirit in the incarnate Son's communion with the Father."[38] The chief worshiper is Jesus Christ, who offers his perfect worship to the Father. Jesus Christ is the "high priest" who "offered himself unblemished to God" so that he would "cleanse our consciences from acts that lead to death, so that we may serve the living God" (Heb 9:1–10). Jesus Christ continues to be our chief worship leader: "he has a permanent priesthood" and "always lives to intercede for" us (Heb 7:24–25). When we gather for worship, the Holy Spirit unites us to our Chief Worshiper. Because we are united to him, we share in his perfect worship of the Father. If we have a God-and-me view worship, there is a temptation to think that our acts of worship earn God's gracious response or, alternately, that our acts of worship are merely *our* response to God's act of grace. However, if we view worship as union with Christ, then we know that our acts of wor-

---

36. Torrance, *Worship, Community*, 20–30.
37. Immink, *Touch of the Sacred*, 26–34.
38. Torrance, *Worship, Community*, 20, 30, 36.

ship do not earn the Father's response of grace—all of the merit is found in Christ. If we view worship as union with Christ, we know that our acts of worship are not simply responses to the God's gift of grace—we know that all that all of our acts of worship are an active participation in Christ by the Holy Spirit.[39]

This means that worship works to bring glory to God. It is effective beyond our wildest imaginations. We sit in the pews for an hour on Sunday morning, mumble through a few songs, and struggle to pay attention as the minister talks. Have you ever thought, "God must be pretty disappointed with me this morning"? God's not. Not if, by the grace of the Holy Spirit, you really are united to Jesus Christ in his perfect worship of the Father. If you are, God the Father is eternally pleased with you and your worship because it is all clothed in the righteousness of Jesus Christ! Your half-hearted mumblings are forgiven. God the Father receives your worship in the perfect worship of Jesus Christ. Worship is union with Christ. Worship—because it is a participation in Christ's worship—is effective at bringing perfect glory to God.

Worship is also effective at forming us because it is union with Christ. Again, we sit in the pews for an hour on Sunday morning, mumble through a few songs, try to pay attention as the minister talks. Have you ever thought, "Maybe I would have been better off going for a run"? Worship seems ineffective. But it's not. Not if worship involves union with Jesus Christ by the Holy Spirit. In that union we are being "united with him in a resurrection like his" (Rom 6:5). Jesus Christ rose from the dead. He has the power to change everything—and that power comes not from us, but from him. And because worship and mission run into each other, as in Ruth Meyers' Möbius strip, we should especially expect that as we worship in union with Christ, we will be formed for our God-given mission in union with Christ: "the church's mission and worship involve participation in Christ."[40]

The rest of this book focuses on discovering missional liturgies that spring from worship in union with Christ. These liturgies are much more than techniques for equipping us for mission, and they are much more than practices that form deep habits in us. These missional liturgies are part of our sanctification, part of our growing up into Christ (Eph 4:12–13), part of our living by his Spirit (Gal 5:16). Missional liturgies are those worship

---

39. Parry, *Worshipping Trinity*, 70–81, 129–46.
40. Davies, *Worship and Mission*, 72.

INTRODUCTION

practices that are both truly worship and truly missional because they are about union with Christ.

It is possible to catalog missional liturgies by working through the parts of a typical order of worship, as many other books have done.[41] Missional prayers are one thing, missional sermons another, and missional celebrations of the sacraments still another. It's also possible to explore what missional liturgy is by considering how mission and worship have intersected throughout history. In the age of the early church, mission and worship came together in one way; at the time of the Reformation, they came together in another.[42] But if worship and mission are both union with Jesus Christ, then missional liturgies can be discovered especially by examining the life and work of Jesus Christ with whom we are united. The seasons of the church year lead us through that life and work. Each season gives us an opportunity to discover a new set practices for worship.

The Plan for This Book

The following chapters explore this missional and liturgical union with Christ according to his birth, his early ministry, his suffering and death, his resurrection, his ascension, and his promised return. These stages in the work of Jesus Christ are celebrated in some of the church's main holidays and seasons, of course. The chapters in this book correspond to seasons in the liturgical calendar. However, you might have already noticed something odd if you looked at the Table of Contents: the first chapter is aimed at Christmas rather than Advent, even though Advent is the traditional beginning of the church year. Ascension and Pentecost are considered in the same chapter, even though they are part of distinct liturgical seasons. That's because this book is guided more by the life and work of Jesus Christ than by the liturgical calendar.

The focus of this book is on missionally transformative worship in union with Christ. Because the seasons of the church year tell the story of the life and work of Jesus Christ, they provide a good pattern with which to explore the various aspects of union with Christ. But it is that union, and not the seasons, that is foundational. Sometimes the seasons touch on more than the life and work of Jesus Christ. For example, Advent involves the anticipation of Christ's first coming and the anticipation of his second coming.

---

41. For example, Schmit, *Sent and Gathered*; and Meyers, *Missional Worship*.
42. For example, Kreider and Kreider, *Worship and Mission*.

But *anticipation* of Christ's first coming doesn't really belong to the life and work of Jesus Christ, properly speaking. The anticipation of the prophets comes *before* his life and work. Pentecost is another example of a festival whose themes branch beyond the life and work of Jesus Christ proper. The focus there is especially on the outpouring of the Holy Spirit. I have written elsewhere about missional worship, the Holy Spirit, and Pentecost,[43] but the focus of this book is on the life and work of Jesus Christ specifically. This book proceeds according to the life and work of Jesus Christ, with the seasons and festivals of the church year providing occasions to consider the various aspects of union with Christ.

It's also the case that I'm writing this book on liturgy and the seasons of the church year from an unlikely place—a tradition and congregation that is only somewhat "liturgical." Congregations in my denomination, the Christian Reformed Church in North America, are varied in their use of the liturgical calendar. The congregations I know well have usually celebrated Christmas, Good Friday, Easter, Ascension Day, and Pentecost. Many observe Advent, some observe Lent, and few observe Epiphany, the Baptism of Jesus, and Trinity Sunday. From my location within the universal Christian church, it makes sense to approach this topic from the side of the stages of the life and work of Jesus Christ rather than from the side of the liturgical calendar.

Each chapter in this book follows the same pattern: First, what does it mean to have union with Christ as he is revealed to us during this stage of his life and work? Second, how does union with him at this stage relate to our mission? And third, what sorts of liturgies can help us worship according to that missional union? The first chapter examines the birth of Jesus Christ and what it means to be united in mission to the Jesus Christ who was incarnate and took on our humble human flesh so that he could give us the divine glory of heaven. Given that union, what might missional liturgy at Christmas be like? The second chapter examines the teaching and miracle ministry of Jesus Christ. What does it mean to be united in mission to Jesus Christ who is Prophet, Priest, and King, and what might related missional liturgy look like? The third chapter focuses on the suffering and death of Jesus, exploring what it means to be united to one who suffered innocently, willingly, and efficaciously. How might liturgy during the season of Lent equip us for mission in union with such a Savior? The fourth chapter examines some of the themes of the resurrection and union with a

---

43. Monsma, "Pentecost and Missional Worship."

INTRODUCTION

risen Jesus Christ—righteousness, new life, and new creation. What does it mean to engage in mission in union with the risen Christ, and what kinds of resurrection-themed liturgies can help us be equipped for that mission? The fifth chapter considers union with Jesus as he ascended to heaven and pours out his Holy Spirit. What does union with him mean for mission, and what kinds of Ascension- and Pentecost-related liturgies might equip us for mission according to that union? The sixth chapter focuses on the promised return of Jesus Christ. We are united to a Savior who has promised to return; we are sent out in mission in union with a coming Savior. How might Advent liturgies equip us for that mission?

You might, of course, read this book through cover-to-cover. But you might also use this book as a kind of seasonal guide. As you prepare for worship during each season of the church year, you might read the chapter for that season to begin thinking about what missional liturgy might mean for that season. However you use it, I hope that you will also gather for worship during each season and be equipped for mission in union with a Christ who was born, taught and performed miracles, suffered, rose, ascended, poured out his Holy Spirit, and promised to return.

one

The Birth of Jesus

It was Christmas Eve, and one church had decorated the front of their worship space with a Christmas scene—a scene complete with a fireplace, stockings, and wrapped gifts underneath a tree. When visitors showed up later that evening, perhaps they would feel at home with the familiar sights of the Christmas holiday. In that comfortable setting, perhaps they would be better able to consider the true meaning of Christmas. In that same neighborhood, each home had received a postcard from another congregation. "Come and join us on Christmas Eve," the mailing read, with lines from familiar Christmas carols. Half of the neighbors hadn't been to church since they were children, except for the occasional baptism or wedding. Perhaps some of them would be drawn by the nostalgia of those Christmas carols. Perhaps they would venture out to hear the classic Christmas sounds of their childhood, the pipe organ swelling with "Hark, the Herald Angels Sing." Down the street, the windows of another church rattled with the sounds of "Happy Birthday," as children practiced to lead the congregation in singing birthday greetings to Jesus later that evening. It might seem like a strange musical choice—certainly not traditional. The hope was that visitors who heard this out-of-place song would find themselves doing more than smiling softly at the sweet songs. Perhaps if they heard a strange musical selection, they would think more deeply about what this holiday was all about. The leadership in these fictional churches planned worship with the mission of God in mind. They hoped that their Christmas Eve worship, with its comfortable décor and familiar hymns or curious song choices, would help their church do its part in the church's mission.

Christmas does offer opportunities to present the gospel to visitors who otherwise would be quite unlikely to step foot in a church. For the past few years, our church has adopted that second strategy. We've made sure that the Christmas Eve service is full of familiar Christmas carols; we've sent postcards out to our neighborhood (or placed ads on social media) inviting our neighbors; I've written the sermon with unbelievers in mind, as though I'm speaking directly to those who are unlikely to hear the gospel any other time of the year. Every year there are a handful of visitors who join us for worship on Christmas Eve, and they hear the gospel.

If we want our churches to bring together Christmas worship and the mission of God, more can be done than simply presenting the gospel to the Christmas-and-Easter worshipers we cajole into our sanctuary. Worship is the spiritual union of the church with Jesus Christ, and Christmas worship becomes union between the Son of God born as a human being and we the human beings who share his human nature. Christmas worship is about being brought into that "marvelous exchange," in which God took on our humanity so that he could bestow his divine gifts on us.[1] Christmas worship is a missional event because the incarnation and the "marvelous exchange" are key pieces of God's mission—that mission of which we are the beneficiaries and that mission in which we are participants. In this chapter, we're going to explore how carefully-prepared liturgies during the Christmas season can help worshipers learn their parts in the mission through union with the Christ who was born in a manger.

United to the Incarnate Christ

The real meaning of Christmas is not the gifts wrapped up under the tree and the filling of stockings hanging by the fireplace, nor is Christmas simply the celebration of the birth of Jesus, the founder of the Christian religion. Christmas is a key event in God's mission and our salvation. It's about the incarnation and that wondrous exchange. To be united to the incarnate Jesus Christ is to have God with you and God for you. Here's what that means:

Matthew and Luke write about the birth of Jesus Christ, and each seems to know that God is with us in the person of Jesus Christ. Matthew looks back at the Old Testament as he begins his gospel. He begins with a genealogy from Abraham to Jesus. He then quotes the Old Testament every few verses, showing that the events of Jesus' birth were fulfilling the Old Testament. Matthew does this to emphasize that the birth of Jesus is all

---

1. The phrase "marvelous exchange" comes from Calvin, *Institutes*, IV.XVII.2.

about God's mission and his faithfulness to his Old Testament promises. To a people who might wonder whether the God of the Old Testament is still with them, the birth of Jesus Christ is a resounding, "Yes!" This presence of the God of the Old Testament, faithful to his promises, is not just for the blood descendants of Abraham. Paul tells us, "If you belong to Christ, then you are Abraham's seed, and heirs according to the promise" (Gal 3:29). Matthew tells us that to be with the Savior born in a manger is to have the God-of-the-past with us.

Luke seems to tell us that to be united to that Savior is to have the God-of-the-future with us. As he begins the story of Jesus Christ, Luke seems focused on God's solutions to injustice. It's as though he is longing for a future when things will be put right. He draws the reader's attention to the politics, powers, and socio-economics of first-century Palestine. The birth of Jesus is an act of peace and justice in the world.[2] For those of us who wonder whether God cares about our oppressed, impoverished, suffering world, Luke seems to be assuring us that because the Savior born in a manger is with us, God is with us.

Rather than telling us the story of the birth of Jesus, John tells us the theology of the incarnation. God is not with us in a mere metaphorical sense. God is not with us just in terms of the themes of a story. Because the Savior born in a manger is with us, *God himself* is with us in the flesh:

> In the beginning was the Word, and the Word was with God, and the Word was God. He was with God in the beginning. Through him all things were made; without him nothing was made that has been made. In him was life, and that life was the light of all mankind. The light shines in the darkness, and the darkness has not overcome it. . . . The Word became flesh and made his dwelling among us. We have seen his glory, the glory of the one and only Son, who came from the Father, full of grace and truth. (John 1:1–5, 14)

One of the themes that will develop later in John's Gospel is the theme of being united to Jesus Christ (especially in chapters 14–16). That theme begins in the very first verses of the Gospel. Before we are united to God, God is united to us. Matthew and Luke hint at it as they look backward and forward, respectively. John makes it clear: to be united to the Jesus Christ who was born in a manger is to have God present with you. That is what it means to have union with an incarnate Jesus Christ: God is with you.

---

2. Green, *Theology of Luke*, 1–16.

The Birth of Jesus

Union with the Savior born in a manger is not just about God being *with* us. It is also about God being *for* us. The "marvelous exchange" shows how God is for us in Jesus Christ. God took upon himself the humility that belongs to us so that we can receive the glory that belongs to God. The apostle Paul teaches us this. Paul writes about the incarnation as a matter of Jesus taking our humility upon himself: Jesus, "being in very nature God, did not consider equality with God something to be used to his own advantage; rather, he made himself nothing by taking the very nature of a servant, being made in human likeness. And being found in appearance as a man, he humbled himself . . ." (Phil 2:6–8). Paul also states the doctrine of the "marvelous exchange" in simple language: "God made him who had no sin to be sin for us, so that in him we might become the righteousness of God" (2 Cor 5:21). In Galatians 4:4, he brings together both the humiliation of Christ in the incarnation and the subsequent exaltation of those who belong to him: "But when the set time had fully come, God sent his Son, born of a woman, born under the law, to redeem those under the law, that we might receive adoption to sonship" (Gal 4:4). God sent his son to us, taking on our humility and the consequences of our sin, so that he might bring us to God to become his children. Union with the Savior born in a manger means not just that God is with us, it also means that God is for us.

I wonder how many of us have worshiped entire Christmas seasons focusing so much on the fact that God is with us that we have neglected to focus on how God is *for* us. Jesus Christ took on human flesh not just so that God would we be with us. He took on human flesh as the first act in a two-part exchange. The incarnation is incomplete without that second part. The reformer John Calvin argued this: "the only reason given in Scripture that the Son of God willed to take our flesh, and accepted this commandment from the Father, is that he would be a sacrifice to appease the Father on our behalf."[3] Calvin expressed this early on in a catechism:

> For he has put on our flesh in order that, being made Son of man,
> he would make us children of God together with himself;
> and, having received on himself our poverty,
> he would transfer his riches to us,
> having taken on himself our weakness,
> he would confirm us by his power;
> having accepted our mortality,

---

3. Calvin, *Institutes*, II.xii.4.

he would give us his immortality;
and being descended to earth,
he would raise us to heaven.⁴

The mission of God is not complete with the incarnation. The mission of God, as God reveals it to us in the birth of Jesus Christ, involves both the incarnation and the "marvelous exchange." Likewise, worship in union with our Christmas Christ means two things for us: it means that God the Son dwelt among us, and it means that God took on our humility so that he could give us the riches of his glory. To be united to the incarnate Jesus Christ is to have God with us and God for us.

Mission in Union with the Incarnate Christ

Through this union with the God who is with us and for us, we are empowered for our part in the church's mission. This empowerment is related both to the incarnation and to the transaction Calvin called "the marvelous exchange." In fact, in the missional-church movement, missional living is often described using incarnation as an analogy. The church sent out on its mission should imitate Jesus Christ in his incarnation, the argument goes: "The Word was made flesh in Jesus, and the church as the body of Christ must continue to be enfleshed in every human culture and moment in mission."⁵ We're united to God the Son who pitched his tent in the middle of our camp. Our mission involves doing the same in our world: pitching our tents in the camps of our neighbors. When a congregation is doing this, you'll notice a few things about their "campsite":

You'll notice that at their campsite, they're using the same kind of camping equipment that others are using. When congregations are engaging in incarnational mission, they learn to talk about the gospel using the language of the locals—they talk about Jesus in ways that their neighbors can readily understand. They learn to live according to the gospel within the customs of their culture—they don't look like complete foreigners. They bridge contexts. They contextualize the gospel. One important skill they have is being able to tell the difference between gospel contextualization, in which they help people in another cultural setting understand

---

4. Calvin, "Calvin's Catechism (1537)," 373. Some of this language would also make its way into *Institutes*, II.xi.2.

5. VanGelder and Zscheile, *Missional Church in Perspective*, 114.

what the gospel means in that context, and cultural imperialism, in which they attempt to make those of another culture more like themselves.[6] Incarnational mission requires humility. In the classic incarnational text in Philippians 2, Paul explicitly calls the church to humility using the example of the incarnation of Jesus Christ. Jesus pitched his tent in our camp, living in human culture and speaking human language that we can understand. In union with him, he sends us to pitch our tents in the camps of our neighbors, living and speaking like them.

You'll also notice at the campsite of a congregation engaged in incarnational mission that the congregation isn't always found in its tent. The campers are spending time at the next campsite over or across the loop. For incarnational mission, it is not good enough to practice hospitality only by inviting others to come to your site. It's not even good enough to practice charity by dropping in now in and then to show a little love to the neighbor. Incarnational mission requires receiving the hospitality of others.[7] We are united to an incarnate Savior who did this. Jesus accepted the hospitality of tax collectors like Matthew (Luke 5:27–29) and Zacchaeus (Luke 19:1–5). Accepting the hospitality of the world was one characteristic of his incarnation, even if the world ultimately refused to be hospitable (John 1:5, 10–11). Those Jesus sends have an obligation to be like him and accept the hospitality of the world (Luke 10). If we're going to pitch our tent in our neighbors' camp, we're going to have to be willing to spend time at their campsite.

Working to contextualize the gospel and being willing to receive hospitality are some of the ways that the church can engage in mission in a way that connects to the doctrine of the incarnation. We do these things because we are united to an incarnate Savior. He did these things, and he sends us out to practice mission the way he did. Our mission includes imitating his incarnation.

This idea—that the incarnation can be used as an analogy for us to imitate—is compelling and useful, but it also suffers some weaknesses.[8] There are two main issues, and they are especially troubling because they show that the incarnation as an analogy is weak right at some of the places it is supposed to be strong. It's supposed to be a strong analogy first because it is supposed to point us to Jesus Christ as our source for good missional

---

6. Hirsch and Catchim, *Permanent Revolution*, 194–95; Keller, *Center Church*, 101–6.

7. VanGelder and Zscheile, *Missional Church in Perspective*, 134.

8. Billings, *Union with Christ*, 123–65; compare to Frost, *The Road to Missional*, 122 and Van Gelder and Zscheile, *Missional Church in Perspective*, 114.

work. Unfortunately, it can become discouraging rather than empowering to look the incarnation as something to imitate. The incarnation was a perfect union of two natures in one person. Jesus is fully God and fully human. If anything like this is the believer's goal in mission, it is an unattainable goal.[9] That can make it discouraging. What church, as it engages in mission, can attain to the perfection of the incarnation? The incarnation is also supposed to be a strong analogy because it teaches us to be humble about our own culture, along the lines of Philippians 2. Paul, however, only suggested a simple comparison of *attitudes*: as Jesus was humble, we should be. Paul didn't suggest there was some incarnational analogy for mission: as Jesus' human nature was to his divine nature, so our . . . ? When a church's mission is compared to the incarnation, it is all too easy to identify the church or its culture with divinity. As an analogy for a congregation's missional work, the incarnation starts suggesting that the congregation should think its own presence and work in the neighborhood is the grace of God.[10] The potential for arrogance is dangerous.

I don't think that comparing our missional work to the incarnation is completely useless. We are sent out in mission in union with the incarnate Jesus Christ. We are to be humble and neighborly like him—and Jesus could only be humble and neighborly because he was incarnate. Our understanding of empowerment for mission in union with the incarnate Jesus Christ, however, needs the kind of corrective that the doctrine of the marvelous exchange can provide. For our missional work, we need to know both of the things that God tells us at Christmas: that he is with us *and* that he is for us. We need to be empowered for mission through union with an incarnate Jesus Christ who performed that wondrous exchange—taking on the humility of our human nature so that he could give us the gift of God's glory. This results in gift-giving mission.

The story of Herod and the Magi shows us how the marvelous exchange changes us. Herod the Great responded to the birth of Jesus Christ by plotting to take Jesus' life. Why? Herod understood that if Jesus was King, then he had come to take something from those in power, like Herod. He had come to take Herod's own royal authority. How would a ruthless King respond to a threat like this? If Jesus threatened to take something from Herod, Herod would threaten to take something from Jesus—his life—and plot to strike first. In contrast, the Magi seemed to understand

---

9. Billings, *Union with Christ*, 125; Tizon, *Missional Preaching*, 40.
10. Billings, *Union with Christ*, 131, 135.

The Birth of Jesus

that if Jesus was King, then he had come to *give* something to them. They responded by giving gifts. What accounts for the difference?

One thing that could account for the difference is an understanding, however rudimentary, of the marvelous exchange in which Christ took on our humility to clothe us with his righteousness. Perhaps the Magi somehow knew that Jesus Christ had come to make that exchange—an exchange that involves not just taking our humility but also giving us the greatest gift. Those who understand this will respond toward God in a certain way—as the Magi did. In fact, they will also respond to the world in a certain way—with a mission characterized by gift-giving.

Theologian Robert P. Sherman describes how God's gift in Jesus Christ transforms interpersonal relationships. God gives us a gift: the life of Jesus Christ to pay the debt we owe to God. Because of this, "Jesus summons us to cease thinking in terms of settling scores, of retribution and revenge, even of 'justice' conceived in distributional terms and to begin thinking in terms of forgiveness, of generosity of spirit, of love even for enemies."[11] You can see the practical consequences of union with the One who made that wondrous exchange in the way a congregation treats the things it finds most precious. Some find their building and grounds precious, others their traditions, or their wealth, or their power, or their time. But when a congregation really knows the gifts God has given them in the gracious exchange through union with Jesus Christ, those precious things seem much less precious in comparison. Soon, they're ready to give those things away for the eternal good of others. In the exchange, God has given the gift of his presence. Knowing this, a congregation is generous with time and visits. In the exchange, God has given the gift of the new creation. Knowing this, a congregation is less protective of and more generous with money and property. In the exchange, God has given the gift of salvation. Knowing this, a church is generous with and eager to share the news of that salvation with others.

In union with the incarnate Jesus Christ, we contextualize the good news and give and receive hospitality in the neighborhood. In union with Jesus Christ who made that loving exchange, we have increased passion for giving gifts—especially the greatest gift, the hope of the gospel—in the midst of this contextualization and hospitality. God is both with us and for us because Jesus Christ was incarnate and made the exchange. In union with him, we are with our neighbors and for our neighbors.

---

11. Sherman, *King, Priest, and Prophet*, 214–15. Keller, *Center Church*, 272, 345.

Missional Liturgy for Christmas

The practices of worship during the Christmas season can be designed to teach worshipers the habits of being with and for their neighbors in union with Jesus Christ. In fact, just worshiping in itself can teach worshipers to be with their culture in union with the incarnate Christ, since the act of worship can imitate the incarnation. The gospel is expressed in preaching, prayer, and song, but clothed in the language and cultural setting of those who have gathered to worship. Those who plan worship do this intentionally: they bring gospel into their cultural context, and they search the cultural riches of their context for treasures that might be received and employed for the worship of God. The very act of worshiping can teach worshipers to expect the gospel to be contextualized, and to be with their culture as God is with their culture.

Liturgy can teach worshipers to be with their culture in other ways—some more direct and some less direct. John D. Witvliet describes some approaches.[12] In some congregations, worship equips the congregation for its work in the world because worship is a break from the bleakness of life in the world. Liturgy is then designed to give a wide-open exposure to the gospel and the glory of God so that worshipers are empowered to live spiritually as they are sent out into the natural world. Other congregations view worship as a subtle preparation for cultural engagement. Liturgy will draw attention to the gospel and the concerns of the world and leave it up to the worshipers to put those things together as they go out to be with the world just as God is in Jesus Christ. Other congregations go a step farther and use worship as a chance to model cultural engagement in the hope that worshipers will participate and learn the habit. Liturgy helps worshipers practice being with the world because the liturgy itself is contextualized in and reciprocates with the local culture.

All of this can happen at any time of the year, but the Christmas season presents special opportunities for liturgy to equip worshipers for being with the world in union with an incarnate Christ. Liturgies that emphasize that God is with us in the incarnation can teach worshipers the habit of noticing how God is with them in their own context, preparing them to notice the same thing for others:

---

12. Witvliet, *Worship Seeking Understanding*, 105–8.

- A prayer for the Lord's Supper: "Lord Jesus, we pray that in this meal you will assure us that you are with us. As surely as you came to be with us in our very human nature when you were born and put in that manger, and as surely as the bread and the wine come to be part of us as they are given to us and placed in our mouths, may you be in us every moment of our lives by your Holy Spirit, wherever we are and whomever we're with . . . ."
- A charge at the conclusion of worship: "God has come to be with the whole world in Jesus Christ. Go out from here to live and speak among the people in your little corner of the world so that they will know that God has come to be with them too."

Practices like these speak about the incarnation and what it means for mission, teaching worshipers to *think* about these things. Other liturgies can lead worshipers to *practice* what the incarnation means for their cultural situation. In some sense, our common Christmas traditions can counteract this—practices like recreating the manger scene (as we imagine it) and even hosting a pageant where children dress in ancient clothing (as we imagine it). Mary and Joseph in robes with a baby born in a manger can make the incarnation seem so exotic or distant. If we are going to learn to expect the gospel to be incarnate in *our* situation, perhaps we need some different practices:

- Have an expectant parent read parts of the story of Jesus' birth.
- Pray for those who will have to endure shame like the shame that Mary and Joseph were about to face—being suspected of marital unfaithfulness.
- Take up an offering for an agency that serves people without homes—people who do not have a bed to sleep in for the night.

Through all of this, continually remind worshipers that in Jesus Christ, God is with us in our situation, whatever it is. When liturgies commemorate the birth of Jesus while noticing the similar situations we are in right now, worshipers might learn the habit of seeing the world as one in which God is with us in the Christ who was incarnate.

Christmas liturgies can also help worshipers learn what it means to go out into the world in union with Jesus Christ who made the marvelous exchange. Liturgies that connect with generosity are suitable. Consider the offering and the Lord's Supper, for example. The offering liturgy often calls to mind the material blessings that God has given the church and the church's thankfulness to God for those blessings. There is a danger, however, that this can allow the worshipers to lose sight of the mission of God and the mission of the church. This can happen if the offering becomes too individualistic. Quiet music is playing, nobody is talking, and each giver fidgets with a wallet and awkwardly folds the cash or check to conceal their giving from their neighbors. The offering is about me and God, and others are not invited into this moment of private worship. Worshipers can also lose sight of God's mission during the offering when the ritual is assumed to be mostly about giving money to the church and other causes to bolster budgets, pay bills, defray expenses, and keep institutions alive. Even more, the words that are said to introduce the offering can point away from the mission of God when the theological content amounts to nothing more than the doctrine of providence: God makes the earth burst forth with goodness and provides us with all that we have. So, let's give to these causes in gratitude.

The Christmas season offers an opportunity to refocus on mission during the offering. When we worship in union with the Savior who made the marvelous exchange, we learn to be generous for a better reason than God's providence. We learn to be generous because of the gospel: God has generously taken our humble humanity on himself to give us his glory. God, generously, has been for us in Jesus Christ. In union with him, we become generous people so that the world can know God's generosity. The worship leader can draw attention to what God is doing through the offering causes, introducing the offering as a prayer—a physically embodied prayer for the work of God's mission.[13] That loving exchange can be mentioned, just as Paul does in 2 Corinthians 8. We give, not just because all gifts come from God but because of "the grace of our Lord Jesus Christ, that though he was rich, yet for your sake he became poor, so that you through his poverty might become rich" (2 Cor 8:9).[14] The offering cause might be introduced by speaking of God's work of bringing the riches of Jesus Christ to the world through the work supported by these gifts: "Let us make this act of collecting our offerings into a prayer—a prayer that God would use this humble organization to bring the riches of his grace in Jesus Christ to the world, just as he has brought eternal riches in the humility of Christ." These liturgies can help to form worshipers for missional generosity.

---

13. Schoon, "Missional Worship"; Lathrop, "Liturgy and Mission," 208–10.
14. Meyers, *Missional Worship*, 188.

The Lord's Supper liturgy also offers an opportunity to form the congregation for missional union with Jesus Christ in whom God is for us in generosity. John Calvin brought the Lord's Supper and the wondrous exchange together in this way:

> Pious souls can derive great confidence and delight from this sacrament, as being a testimony that they form one body with Christ, so that everything which is his they may call their own. . . . This is the wondrous exchange made by his boundless goodness. Having become with us the Son of Man, he has made us with himself sons of God. By his own descent to the earth he has prepared our ascent to heaven. Having received our mortality, he has bestowed on us his immortality. Having undertaken our weakness, he has made us strong in his strength. Having submitted to our poverty, he has transferred to us his riches. Having taken upon himself the burden of unrighteousness with which we were oppressed, he has clothed us with his righteousness.[15]

This kind of description can become part of the Lord's Supper liturgy, as has happened in the Dutch Reformed tradition:

> . . . he was bound that we might be loosed from our sins; that afterwards he suffered innumerable reproaches that we might never be confounded, that he was innocently condemned to death that we might be acquitted at the judgment seat of God . . . and so has taken the curse from us upon himself that he might fill us with his blessing; and has humbled himself unto the very deepest reproach and anguish of hell, in body and soul, on the tree of the cross, when he cried out with a loud voice: "My God, my God, why hast thou forsaken me?" that we might be accepted of God, and nevermore be forsaken of him . . . .[16]

In addition, the Lord's Supper liturgy can conclude with a kind of commissioning of those who will bring the elements to others who were unable to attend worship.[17] This is a liturgical act of participating in Jesus Christ as he is for us and our world. The liturgy can even emphasize the time that those delivering the elements will give up in order to deliver the means of grace. In union with Jesus Christ who made that marvelous exchange, we are generous with the things we find most precious because

15. Calvin, *Institutes*, IV.xvii.2.
16. "Form for the Lord's Supper," 91.
17. Meyers, *Missional Worship*, 183–85.

we know how generous God has been, giving us his glory by taking upon himself our humanity.

When the marvelous exchange becomes part of liturgies that focus on giving, we learn generosity in Jesus Christ. He was the one who took on our humility so that he could give us the gift of his glory. In union with him, we are sent out to be generous.

In these ways, liturgies during the Christmas season can help worshipers learn the habits of mission in union with the incarnate Jesus Christ. Worshipers can be empowered for incarnational living through liturgies that focus on the incarnation and that model incarnational contextualization and reciprocal hospitality. Worshipers can be empowered for humble generosity through liturgies that focus on the loving and love-inspiring exchange, especially during the offering and the Lord's Supper. This connection between mission and Christmas worship goes far beyond using increased Christmas attendance for another gospel appeal (although that's a good thing, too).

two

The Peripatetic Ministry of Jesus

IMAGINE THIS: THE TIME has come to pray with the young children and dismiss them for Children's Worship. I invite them forward and take out a board book. (You know the kind: brightly-colored with one sentence on each of the ten thick cardboard pages.) I begin reading a colorful children's version of one of Jesus' parables, *The Foolish Farmer*.[1] Then, as I turn and show them one of the last pages, I read: "'You fool,' said God. 'Tonight you will die. Who will get your money now?'"

In our church, you'd have to just imagine that scene; you couldn't witness it, because it hasn't happened yet. I haven't had the courage to read *that* particular book to the kids. I have a collection of Carine Mackenzie's "Stories Jesus Told" board books, and I like the idea of reading them as part of the prayer with the children in worship now and then. But I'm not about to use the one about the foolish farmer. It seems a little too brutal, too morbid, too stark for children, doesn't it? I have this sense deep inside that the stories we tell children from the Bible should be cute. Maybe you do too.

Especially when we are telling Bible stories to children, many of us want to skip over the details that aren't cute. We go out of our way to tell the cute little details of the Christmas story—the baby, the animals, and the shepherds, but we don't usually go out of our way to tell the next story: the one about Herod's slaughter of the innocent baby boys in Bethlehem. We teach about the miraculous protection of Shadrach, Meshach, and Abednego in the fiery furnace. But do we tell them that Nebuchadnezzar issued a decree that anyone who defamed the God of Shadrach, Meshach, and Abednego would be cut into pieces?

1. Mackenzie, *The Foolish Farmer*.

Worship, Mission, and the Church Year

God didn't give us the Bible as a collection of cute stories. The Bible shows us salvation. In the parable of the foolish farmer, Jesus is warning us about fleeting nature of worldly possessions in comparison to the eternal value of the kingdom. The manger scene in the Christmas story is not about cute sheep, but about the self-humbling Son of God. The stories of Daniel, his friends, and the others during the exile and the return are often about the ambiguous nature of political powers who are friendly toward God's people: rather than trusting earthly powers to promote our spiritual well-being, we need to turn our hearts to God. The Bible has some difficult and challenging parts, of course, and these need to be taught to children in age-appropriate ways. But however we teach the stories, let's not pretend that God has given us an anthology of cute fables. The Bible shows us salvation.

That's easy to see with many of the stages of Jesus' life and work. His birth shows us the incarnation. His death and resurrection shows us forgiveness. His ascension and promised return show us his victory. However, it can be harder to see salvation in some of the stories of Jesus' ministry from his baptism up until his entry into Jerusalem. I'll call this the *peripatetic* ministry of Jesus (from a Greek word that means "walking around"). The stories of Jesus' peripatetic ministry are varied. There are miracles and tender moments of mercy. Jesus teaches and rebukes. The events and parables are often vivid and fun to tell. Sometimes, it might be easier to focus on how cute they are than to see salvation in them. Even worse, in many of our churches, we skip over the peripatetic ministry of Jesus altogether—at least in our worship. We might study some of these stories in Sunday School and Bible studies. But in worship, these can be some of the most neglected events in the life and work of Jesus Christ.

Maybe I'm just being autobiographical. The time between Christmas and Lent—sometimes the whole season is given the name "Epiphany"—is perfect for a focus on the peripatetic ministry. The *Revised Common Lectionary* suggests many of these stories during this season. However, in my church, while we celebrate Christmas every year and turn to repentance and the suffering and death of Jesus during Lent, I have typically diverted attention away from the story of Jesus' earthly ministry to some other theme in the interim. For several years, one dear older woman took me aside at the end of January and asked if I was going preach on Epiphany and the baptism of Jesus next year. She wanted a season to worship around the themes of Jesus' peripatetic ministry. But, by the end of January, she realized that, once again, I had planned something else. Eventually she took me aside in November, and that worked. I did it. After Christmas, I preached on the escape to Egypt, the baptism of Jesus, the calling of the disciples, and the teaching and miracle-working ministry of Jesus. For her sake, I'm glad I did. It turned out to be her last chance, as she died later that year.

I now look around at the people I worship with each Sunday, and I think: *Let's make sure we worship with those stories long before the last years of our lives.* We need to travel with Jesus, so to speak, as he teaches and performs his miracles. We need to meet the flesh-and-blood Jesus who traveled the land of Judea and Samaria. We need to experience what it is like to worship the one who calmed the storm and drove out demons, to listen to the Bible read as though our sandaled Savior was speaking the words, to eat from the table of the one who tenderly loved sinners and tax-collectors. All of us need to rehearse the stories of Jesus' peripatetic ministry in worship, and not because the stories are cute. Rehearsing the stories of salvation in worship helps us to learn the habits of union with the Savior for the rest of our lives. Specifically, worshiping with these stories can help us learn three missional habits:

- broad engagement in missional work,
- relying on the perfect work of Jesus, and
- treating the proclamation of the gospel as the ultimate thing.

United to the Messiah

How exactly can the scattered stories of sermons and miracles teach us these missional habits? Before I suggest an answer, I have some homework for you: set this book down for a little while and go read the first part of one of the Gospels, up until the entry of Jesus into Jerusalem. Notice who Jesus is.

(Go do it now.)

So, who is Jesus? His brothers seem to have regarded him primarily as a miracle-worker (John 7:1–5). Frustrated with the growing opposition to their brother and struggling with their own doubts about him, they encouraged Jesus to ply his wares as a miracle worker at the Feast of Tabernacles. Is that how you think of Jesus during his ministry on earth? As a miracle worker? Or do you think of him primarily as one who forgives sins? That's the crime he was often accused of (for example, Mark 2:7), claiming the authority that only God has—the authority to forgive sins. Or do you think of him as a teacher, a rabbi? His disciples often gave him that title (for example, Mark 9:5). Is it is his power to perform miracles, his profound teaching, or his calls to repentance and assurance of forgiveness that stand out to you?

If you did your homework, maybe you noticed the wild variety in the kinds of things Jesus did. I just finished reading through the Gospels as part of reading through the whole Bible in a year. What struck me about Jesus' peripatetic ministry was exactly this: in contrast to Old Testament prophets and figures, Jesus does all sorts of things. Some prophets in the Old Testament stand out for their vivid preaching, others for their graphic symbolic actions, still others for their miraculous signs. But Jesus does it all. In one paragraph he's exercising miraculous power, in the next he's telling a parable that strikes right at our hearts, and in the next he's lovingly assuring an outcast of forgiveness. Jesus does *all* of it.

He does all of it because our salvation is all of it—and his peripatetic ministry shows us the breadth of our salvation. You might have thought of salvation as primarily a matter of finding the person you can truly trust. You might have thought of salvation as being assured that your Creator forgives you. You might have thought of salvation as hope for a troubled world. All of that is good, but if you thought of salvation as *only* one of those things, if you have tended to neglect other aspects of God's saving work in Jesus Christ, you've been missing out. And you've been missing out not just on *thinking* a certain way about salvation. You're missing out on *acting* a certain way as a person who is saved. You need *all* the stories of Jesus' peripatetic ministry. Together, they show us the breadth of salvation. Together, they show us the breadth of the church's mission. These scattered stories can teach us those three missional habits because the stories reveal that Jesus Christ is the Messiah, the Prophet, Priest, and King, and we are united to him.

Jesus the Prophet, Priest, and King

Jesus was a teacher. He also loved and forgave with the mercy of God. He even worked miracles with power over demons, the forces of nature, and the laws of physics. There is a biblical concept that ties all of this together: Jesus is the anointed one, "Messiah" in Hebrew and "Christ" in Greek. And this Messiah holds three offices—the offices of Prophet, Priest, and King. This is, ultimately, what the stories of his peripatetic ministry show us.

The Peripatetic Ministry of Jesus

We see this at his baptism first. The accounts of Jesus' baptism are almost identical: Jesus is immersed in the River Jordan, the Spirit descends on him like a dove, and a voice from heaven quotes from the Psalms, naming him the Son of God. These three things mark Jesus as the one who holds the office of the Messiah, fulfilling the Old Testament offices of Prophet, Priest, and King. The prophets of the Old Testament were anointed with the Holy Spirit, and Jesus is visibly anointed in a way as the Spirit descends on him like a dove. Later, Jesus confirms this "anointing with the Spirit" interpretation of his baptism, as he applies to himself Isaiah 61: "The Spirit of the Lord is on me, because he has anointed me to proclaim good news to the poor . . ." (Luke 4:18). Jesus is anointed as the Prophet. When the voice names him the "Son," we also hear that Jesus is the King. He's the king that the Old Testament spoke of—the descendant of David. Psalm 2 is ostensibly about David, but as the Father's voice thunders from heaven at the Jordan River—"You are my Son" (Mark 1:11)—we understand that the psalm is really about the King of Kings. The anointed eschatological King, the Messiah, is spoken of elsewhere in the Psalms, such as in Psalm 110, where the king sits at the right hand of the Father. Psalm 110 notably also calls him a priest. In Israel, those holding the offices of king and priest were anointed with oil (see 1 Samuel 10 and 16 and Exodus 28). There's no oil at Jesus' baptism, but when Jesus is confirmed by that voice as the King and the Priest, we see some of the significance of his baptism with water: he's been anointed with water just as he was anointed with Spirit. He is the Messiah, the Prophet, Priest, and King.

Theologian Robert Sherman suggests that the temptations Jesus endures after his baptism also reflect this threefold office as Messiah.[2] The three temptations test precisely those three dimensions of his work—as Prophet, Priest, and King. In the desert, Jesus is tempted to abuse his prophetic office, using his prophetic power to satisfy his hunger by producing miraculous food just as the first prophet, Moses, had. Jesus resists, and names the true calling of a prophet—to proclaim the word by which alone human beings live. At the pinnacle of the temple, Jesus is tempted to abuse his priestly office, appealing to his role as God's chosen one to save his life at the site of the sacrifices. Instead, Jesus knows that his priestly role is to give his life as the true sacrifice, and he resists the temptation. On the mountain, Jesus is tempted to abuse his kingly office, submitting to the devil to take a shortcut to worldwide rule. Jesus resists, for his kingly reign requires dying,

---

2. Sherman, *King, Priest, and Prophet*, 110–15.

rising, and ascending. Sherman acknowledges that this interpretation of the temptations is unusual. It is compelling, however.

It becomes even more compelling once you start to notice how everything that Jesus does can be tied to one of these three dimensions of his office as Messiah. After telling of the anointing of Jesus at his baptism and the subsequent three temptations, Matthew offers three quick stories that serve as a kind of summary of the work Jesus will do during his peripatetic ministry. The stories are like movie previews, foreshadowing the sorts of things that the reader will encounter in the rest of the peripatetic ministry. Frederick Dale Bruner correlates these three acts of ministry in the last half of Matthew 4 with the three temptations. The temptations show how Jesus should *not* minister, he argues, and the three acts that follow show how he *should* and *will* minister.[3] If the three temptations reflect his threefold messianic office as Prophet, Priest, and King, do these three foreshadowing acts of ministry also reflect that threefold office? They seem to.

First, according to the prophetic dimension of his office, Jesus preaches (Matt 4:17). This corresponds to the temptation to make his ministry about something other than the word of God (Matt 4:4). Second, according to priestly dimension of his office, Jesus acts to save others, making his disciples "fishers of men" (Matt 4:19). This corresponds to the temptation to make his ministry about the salvation of himself (Matt 4:6). Third, according to the kingly dimension of his office, Jesus exercises power over the enemies of God, healing the sick (Matt 4:24). This corresponds to the temptation to cede this authority to the devil so that he could exercise a subordinate rule over the world (Matt 4:9). These three previews correspond to the three dimensions of his office as Messiah. And keep reading: everything he does can be traced back through one of these three initial acts of ministry, through one of his temptations, to his baptism, where he is anointed as Messiah—Prophet, Priest, and King.

I've been fascinated with the threefold office of Jesus Christ for some time, and I've noticed that it is possible to find it almost everywhere in the Bible. For example, faith, hope, and love each correspond to a dimension of the threefold office: faith to the prophetic, hope to the kingly, and love to the priestly.[4] On the one hand, that's a reason to be careful. You and I each

---

3. Bruner, *Matthew*, 117–18.

4. Dutch theologian Herman Bavinck, following his contemporary Abraham Kuyper, suggested that the three dimensions of Christ's office have their ground in creation and human nature itself: "The truth is that the idea of humanness already encompasses within itself this threefold dignity and activity. Human beings have a head to know,

have a human brain, a biological tool that is typically good at seeing patterns. In fact, sometimes our brains are *too* good at seeing patterns, so that we see patterns where there are none. Maybe I'm seeing Christ's threefold office everywhere in Scripture because I *expect* to see it everywhere. Maybe it isn't really there. On the other hand, this idea of Christ's threefold office has deep historical roots,[5] and it does provide a good, biblical way of understanding the breadth of what Jesus was up to. If you want to understand how the varied stories of Jesus' peripatetic ministry show us salvation in its breadth, this is a great way. In all of this, Jesus is revealed as the Prophet, Priest, and King that God has sent us. He is the Messiah.

United to the Prophet, Priest, and King

The threefold office of Jesus as the Messiah also points to three ways we should be changed by union with the Messiah. Jesus' anointing was an anointing of water and Spirit. We who are baptized and put our faith in Jesus Christ have also received that anointing. There should be a threefoldness to our Christian living in union with the Messiah.

I once preached a sermon in which I referred repeatedly to "little messiahs," drawing on the title David often gave King Saul: "the Lord's anointed" (that is, "the Lord's messiah"). I suspected some of the congregation would be a little bit anxious with me calling someone other than Jesus Christ a "messiah." I wasn't wrong. At least one person was uncomfortable with that language, and he told me so afterward. I'm sure there were a few others who furrowed their brows as I preached, even calling them "little messiahs."

When I preached that sermon, I was prepared for questions. Jesus is the one Messiah. He is the only Savior. His anointing is unique. But all of us who belong to him are also anointed ones with a lesser anointing, "christs" in Greek, "messiahs" in Hebrew. I was ready to point to a piece of our church's confessions. The Heidelberg Catechism says this after discussing the threefold office of Christ:

---

a heart to give themselves, a hand to govern and to lead; correspondingly, they were in the beginning equipped by God with knowledge and understanding, with righteousness and holiness, with dominion and glory . . ." (*Reformed Dogmatics*, vol. 3, 367). Even the Heidelberg Catechism seems to recognize this threefold activity in human nature created in the image of God: God created human beings in his own image "so that they might truly know God their creator, love him with all their heart, and live with God in eternal happiness . . ." (Q&A 6).

5. Sherman, *King, Priest, and Prophet*, 63–76.

Worship, Mission, and the Church Year

Q. 32. But why are you called a Christian?

A. 32. Because by faith I am a member of Christ, and so I share in his anointing. I am anointed

- to confess his name,
- to present myself to him as a living sacrifice of thanks,
- to strive with a free conscience against sin and the devil in this life, and afterward to reign with Christ over all creation for eternity.[6]

The bulleted clauses in the quotation above correspond to Christ's prophetic, priestly, and kingly offices, respectively. We share in the anointing of the Anointed One. We have a calling to be prophetic, priestly, and kingly.

What is our prophetic work in union with the Prophet? We "confess his name," the Heidelberg Catechism says. We are called and enabled by the Spirit to know the truth by faith and to speak the truth in praise to God.[7] Of course, Jesus Christ is *the* Prophet. He is the prophecy itself, the Word, and he is the one who gives the Spirit, the one who enables us to proclaim the truth from our hearts.[8] Think about this: if we had to profess faith without being united to the Messiah, our faith would be too weak to be saving faith. If we had to worship God without union with Christ, our worship would be too corrupted by sin to bring God glory. However, our faith is saving faith and our praise does bring God glory. How? Through union with the Messiah who is Prophet and Prophecy. The worship of our minds and mouths is perfected only by the Messiah's perfection.

What is our priestly work? The Bible teaches that the church is a "holy priesthood" (1 Pet 2:5). As a holy priesthood, we no longer offer sacrifices of atonement, but we do offer sacrifices of thanksgiving—living sacrifices, in fact. Our priestly work doesn't include offering animal sacrifices, because we are priests in union with the priestly work of the Messiah, who offered his own life as the final sacrifice for the forgiveness of sins: "by one sacrifice he has made perfect forever those who are being made holy . . . where these have been forgiven, sacrifice for sin is no longer necessary" (Heb 10:14, 18). Because we only do priestly work in union with this High Priest, we don't offer the sacrifices that he has ended, but we do offer ourselves, alive, as sacrifices of thanks to him. We do this now not because we hope to be right with God, but because he has already made us right with God. John Calvin

---

6. "Heidelberg Catechism," Q&A 32.
7. Billings, *Union with Christ*, 162–3; Ursinus, *Commentary*, 179.
8. Sherman, *King, Priest, and Prophet*, 256–61.

explained it this way: to be united to this Priest and share in his priestly anointing means that we have inner peace, that we pray confidently and worship exuberantly as we boldly approach the throne of God.[9]

Our kingly work is also done through union with Jesus Christ. Paul writes that we who have received God's abundant grace "reign in life through the one man, Jesus Christ" (Rom 5:17). Reigning in life means that we live in victory over the forces of sin, temptation, and evil. We resist these forces in an anticipation of our eternal freedom from them. We do this not because we are strong but because we are united to the Victor, the Messiah. We can only resist temptation and fight with perseverance against the forces of evil because we know that we have been set free by the Messiah from our bondage to sin and because the forces of evil against which we strive are already defeated by the Messiah.

It is important for us to spend more time in worship with the stories of the peripatetic ministry of Jesus because, in worshiping the Prophet, Priest, and King, we learn the habits of professing faith, praising God, praying boldly, confessing and having confidence that we're forgiven, living to the glory of God, and resisting temptation and evil with perseverance. We learn those habits through the conscious and subconscious realities of union with Christ. It's hard, for example, to have stories of a cute miracle-worker change our lives, even if we know that he is in us and we are in him. But a Savior who has power over all creation, even the forces of evil that torment us? Our lives are changed when we walk around knowing that we are united to the Messiah who walked around showing us the breadth of our salvation in his peripatetic ministry.

Mission in Union with the Messiah

So far, I've described the work we do in union with the Messiah mostly in terms of an internal or private relationship between ourselves and God. I've said that our prophetic work in union with the anointed Prophet is professing faith and giving praise. That's mostly about us and God. I've said that our priestly work in union with the anointed Priest is confessing our sins and praying boldly, but that also is mostly about us and God. Our kingly work in union with the anointed King is about resisting temptation and obeying God, but (you guessed it) that's mostly about us and God. Union with Christ, however, is not only about us and God, and when we look at

---

9. Calvin, *Institutes*, II.xv.6; Ursinus, *Commentary*, 179–80.

the peripatetic ministry of Jesus Christ, we don't just see our salvation (what Jesus does for our personal relationships with God), we see the mission of God and his church (what Jesus does for the world). Rehearsing the stories of Jesus' peripatetic ministry in worship is as much about learning the habits of Christian devotion as it is about learning the habits of the mission of the church. There are three habits, mentioned earlier, to pay attention to:

- engaging broadly in the mission,
- relying on the perfect work of Jesus, and
- treating the proclamation of the gospel as the ultimate thing.

Engaging Broadly in the Mission

Worship in union with Christ, the Prophet, Priest, and King, teaches us a first missional habit: engaging broadly in the mission that God has given us. The classic theologians of the Protestant Reformation are sometimes criticized for ignoring the missional dimension of Christian faith—this sense that our union with Christ is *for the world*. Theologian Renee S. House objects to this criticism. The Heidelberg Catechism, for example, describes participation in the threefold office of the Messiah as a missional thing.[10] When that catechism says that we share in the anointing of our Prophet, Priest, and King, the authors had in mind a missional union with Christ. Zacharias Ursinus, one of its principal authors, wrote that our sharing in the prophetic office of Christ means that the name of Christ would be professed in every place, and our sharing in the priestly office of Christ is about revealing God to others and offering prayers and offerings—which are, of course, not just for us, but for others. Our sharing in the kingly office of Christ is a matter of opposing and overcoming "the devil, the world, and all enemies."[11] Union with the Messiah, the Prophet, Priest, and King, is as much about how we go to the world as it is about how we come to God. We are supposed to be prophetic, priestly, and kingly as we make our way through life.

Most people, whether they have faith in Jesus Christ or not, have a sense that this is true: we're supposed to engage in a broad range of good works as we go out into the world. We're supposed to speak the truth, seek

---

10. House, "Becoming a 'Missional' Denomination," 315–16.
11. Ursinus, *Commentary*, 179.

to be at peace with people, and work for what is good. God has left this remnant of his image in our hearts, this knowledge that we're supposed to be like the Messiah—not just prophets, not just priests, not just kings, but all of it. And many people make good efforts to be truth-tellers, reconciliation-seekers, and doers of good works. Sometimes, I'm embarrassed by the fact that others outside the church seem to understand some of this better than we who are inside. I see or hear about some secular or non-Christian group that seems to be doing a better job of some important work in the world than the Christians who have set out to do similar work. I shake my head, but the fact is that we were created to know, at least in a small way, what the work of Jesus Christ even more clearly shows us: that God's work in the world is broad. When we worship in union with the peripatetic Christ, we learn the habit of engaging broadly in that missional work.

Relying on the Perfect Work of Jesus Christ

Worship in union with the anointed Jesus teaches us to rely on his perfect work rather than on our own efforts. Even those with the best intentions to do these good works never quite measure up to God's standard. Even the best good works, specifically when done apart from faith in Jesus Christ, are not in themselves good enough for God's saving mission. When we realize how feeble our good works are, our natural response is one of two things: either we narrow the scope of our work to something more manageable, or we doubt that success is possible at all. In a certain way, rehearsing the stories of Jesus' peripatetic ministry teaches us a different solution to the problem. The more we walk with the Messiah, the more we learn about the centrality of the work of the Messiah. We learn that the mission is possible because it is finally accomplished not through our work, but through the work of the one Anointed One, the Messiah.

The Messiah is the Prophet, the Prophecy, and the one who gives us the power to proclaim his word as he pours out his Spirit on us. This changes our talking about the gospel as much as it changes our faith in the gospel. The only reason you can tell someone else the good news in a powerful, personal, and life-changing way is through union with the Messiah. It's not because you can imitate the Messiah, hoping to somehow be as persuasive as he was. You can't. Just read the stories of the calling of those first disciples: "'Come, follow me,' Jesus said, 'and I will send you out to fish for people.' At once they left their nets and followed him" (Mark 1:17–18).

Who of us could have that kind of impact on someone's life? Only the Messiah. As you speak to others, telling the good news, rely on him to reveal himself by the power of his Holy Spirit.[12]

When you go out into the world to engage in the priestly work of revealing the grace of God to others while you reconcile yourself with them, you don't have to do this by mustering up the right kind of priestly energy. Priestly work, at its heart, is intercessory work. The priest makes God known to the people and brings the people's prayers to God. You have a calling to do something similar in the world: to make God's grace known through love and reconciliation and to bring prayers of intercession on behalf of the world to a listening God. But how hard it is to give generously and to love others deeply when we're not sure they deserve it! How hard it is to seek reconciliation with people when we must humble ourselves first! How hard it is to pray real prayers of intercession for truly awful people! This is all so hard—impossible actually—that some of us give up. We stop trying to do this priestly work in our world, or we doubt that it can be done with any success. It is impossible, except through union with the Messiah. We experience true love only in his love for us. He is the one who has already accomplished reconciliation—the kinds of wrongs you have a hard time forgiving are straightforwardly forgiven by the forgiveness of Christ. You bring your messy prayers to God in the confidence of his completed sacrifice on your behalf.

The victory of the King Jesus Christ is necessary if you're going to do the kind of missional kingly work that God calls you to: going out into the world to fight against sin, death, and evil. You need to be united to the one who has already won victory over those things if you're going to resist narrowing the scope of your kingly calling or giving up altogether. You'll never have the right combination or humility and confidence, unless you know that you won't win the victory, but the Messiah already has in his kingly office. The kingdom is not something we are trying to create. It is something that Christ has established in his victory. Believers only work to make it known, to participate in it, and to enjoy glimpses of it.

The peripatetic ministry of Jesus Christ shows us that the work is accomplished by the Messiah. If we want to have ambition, perseverance, confidence, and hope in the church's mission, we need to spend more time

---

12. See Calvin, *Institutes*, II.xv.2, specifically commenting on preaching: "[H]e received anointing, not only for himself that he might carry out the office of teaching, but for his whole body that the power of the Spirit might be present in the continuing preaching of the gospel."

with the stories of Jesus teaching, forgiving, and healing. We need to spend more time learning consciously and subconsciously that Jesus Christ is the Messiah. That's how we learn the habit of relying on the perfect work of Jesus.

Treating Proclamation of the Gospel as the Ultimate Thing

Finally, worship that orients us to the peripatetic ministry of Christ teaches us to treat the proclamation of the gospel and the goal of leading people to respond with faith in Jesus as the ultimate thing. It's not just that *we* need to know, deep inside, that Christ's work is sufficient as we go out into the world. We should want *others* to come to know that Christ's work is sufficient. That is what is ultimate in the mission of the church. Pastors Kevin DeYoung and Greg Gilbert agree, even arguing that things like social justice are *not* the church's mission:

> . . . the mission of the church is to go into the world and make disciples by declaring the gospel of Jesus Christ in the power of the Spirit and gathering these disciples into churches, that they might worship and obey Jesus Christ now and in eternity to the glory of God the Father. In contrast to recent trends, we've tried to demonstrate the mission is not everything God is doing in the world, nor the social transformation of the world or our societies, nor everything we do in obedience to Christ. (italics in original)[13]

In contrast, others disagree, like theologian Michal Frost, who argues that attaching some priority to the proclamation of the gospel is foolish:

> [E]vangelism and social involvement are so entwined that it is folly to try to unravel them. They are both equally important and equally necessary expressions of this marvelous task of alerting people to the reign of God. Trying to determine which has priority and which should take precedence is impossible.[14]

Should we go as far as DeYoung and Gilbert, saying that *only* proclamation is the mission of the church? Or should we go as far as Frost on the other side, saying that all of the things we are sent out to do are *equally* the mission of the church?

---

13. DeYoung and Gilbert, *What is the Mission*, 241.
14. Frost, *The Road to Missional*, 28.

DeYoung and Gilbert rely on a distinction between the church as an organization—the local church and the denomination—and believers in general. The mission of believers in general is that broad mission, but the mission of the church as an organization is making disciples through the proclamation of the gospel. Even DeYoung and Gilbert recognize that, in some ways, this distinction is too tidy. It's just not possible to separate out some aspects of the mission and assign them to the church as an organization and others to believers in general.[15] For example, effectively proclaiming the gospel might require that the church as organization mobilize members to respond to a social issue, like abortion or immigration. It would be problematic and would undermine prophetic work if the church as organization refused to engage in this kind of kingly work—working against injustice and evil in the world. Rather than answering this question with a strict distinction between the organization and the organism of the church, it is better to recognize that the proclamation of the gospel, the participation in Christ's prophetic office, has a special position in the work that the church must do. In fact, I'm convinced that this is true not only for the church as an organization, but for Christians in general.

How should we describe this special position? Should we say that proclaiming the good news is most important or primary? We don't want to suggest that things other than evangelism are less important, as though we can be happy if we fail to love our neighbors as long as we did the "most important thing": evangelize to them. Nor do we want to suggest that we can engage in priestly or kingly work among our neighbors only *after* we have first preached the gospel to them. Instead, missiologist Christopher Wright suggests that we describe the special position of evangelism using the word "ultimate":

> Mission may not always *begin* with evangelism. But mission that does not ultimately *include* declaring the Word and the name of Christ, the call to repentance, and faith and obedience has not completed its task. It is defective mission, not holistic mission.[16]

What does it look like for evangelism to be ultimate in our other work? A friend of mine told me about his church's involvement in a community effort to promote health one weekend. The members of their congregation were so visible at the event that he was interviewed by the local news media.

---

15. DeYoung and Gilbert, *What is the Mission*, 232–33.
16. Wright, *Mission of God*, 319.

They asked why his church was involved. He was excited to explain that they were involved in this as a church because they know that God loves life. In fact, they believe that God loves life so much that he died to give us life forever.

The ultimacy of gospel proclamation is one reason why we need to rehearse the stories in worship of Jesus' peripatetic ministry more. If we try to do all this good work without the stories of the Messiah's work as Prophet, Priest, and King swirling in our heads and residing in our bones, we'll never be prepared to give an answer like that. We won't have developed the habit of making the good news of Jesus Christ ultimate in what we do. But when we worship in a way that points us toward union with the Messiah, we learn the habit of treating the proclamation of the gospel as the ultimate thing.

Missional Liturgy for the Peripatetic Ministry

The season between Christmas and Lent is the perfect time to worship using the stories of Jesus' peripatetic ministry. Worship at this time can reinforce those three missional habits: engaging broadly in prophetic, priestly, and kingly work in the world; relying on the perfect work of the Messiah as we engage in that threefold work; and treating the proclamation of the gospel as ultimate in the church's mission. Here are some liturgies that are especially fitting if we are hoping for the Holy Spirit to form those habits in us during this season.

Call to Worship

The Messiah gathers the church for worship just as he sends us out for our mission. It might be obvious that if the *sending* liturgy reminds us that the perfect Prophet, Priest, and King is sending us out in union with him, our habit of relying on Christ can be reinforced. But what about the gathering liturgy, the call to worship? The same habit can be reinforced with gathering liturgies that use Jesus' own priestly words as a call to worship, perhaps introduced with words that connect these words to our world's need for a priest:

- "The world is weighed down by the burden of doing the right thing, convinced it is failing. To this world, Jesus says, 'Come to me, all you who are weary and burdened, and I will give you rest. Take my yoke upon you and learn from me, for I am gentle and humble in heart, and you will find rest for your souls. For my yoke is easy and my burden is light'" (Matt 11:28–30).

- "Jesus gathers people who feel neglected, ignored, overlooked, and insignificant, saying, 'Let the little children come to me, and do not hinder them, for the kingdom of heaven belongs to such as these'" (Matt 19:14).

The call to worship can also highlight Jesus' kingly power, displayed through his miracles. I've often used a story from the life of Jesus Christ as the call to worship during Advent, or on Palm Sunday or Easter, but the stories of Jesus' miracles are appropriate for this too, to reinforce the habit of relying on Jesus as the perfect king:

- Read an account of Jesus driving out an impure spirit, from Mark 1:21–28, for example, and say: "This Messiah calls us, people who live in a world tormented by evil, to worship him this morning."
- Read an account of Jesus performing a miraculous healing, from Mark 1:29–31, for example, and say: "This Messiah calls a world dying from disease and sickness to worship him."
- Read an account of Jesus performing miracle of power over the forces of nature, from Mark 4:35–41, for example, and say: "This Messiah calls us to worship him, as gathers us from our work of fighting against forces beyond our control."

Any of these can be incorporated with the reading or singing of an appropriate psalm. For example, a reading about Jesus calming the wind and the waves, can be paired with Psalm 29: "The voice of the Lord is over the waters . . ." (verse 3).

Confession and Assurance

The liturgy of confession and assurance is a natural time to highlight the priestly work of the Messiah and the fact that it is not just our being forgiven that happens in union with him, but our forgiving others, also. Liturgies can reinforce the habits of engaging in priestly work as part of our mission. Some congregations might tend to think of the mission of the church as limited to evangelism. Worshipers in these churches can be reminded that our mission is not only to preach to our neighbors, but also to forgive them. For example:

- The story of the woman caught in adultery (John 8) can be used as a call to confession, pointing out that we are quick to join in condemning others. If the Messiah can forgive them, surely we should.
- A prayer of confession based on the petition "forgive us our debts," which Jesus taught us to say during his peripatetic ministry, can be followed with the teaching of Jesus on how we should live as people who know that we are forgiven: "For if you forgive other people when they sin against you, your heavenly Father will also forgive you. But if you do not forgive others their sins, your Father will not forgive your sins" (Matt 6:14–15).

The confession and assurance can also help to reinforce the habit of gospel centrality and relying on the perfect priestly work of the Messiah. Congregations that tend to think of mission in expansive terms, especially when it is assumed that the gospel will be proclaimed through good works, might benefit from something like this:

- After confessing our reluctance to do the priestly work of forgiving others, the assurance of pardon can take place from a baptismal font, connecting our baptism with the baptism of Jesus. Hearing of forgiveness while being physically reminded of the union between our baptism and the baptism of our Messiah can reinforce in us the habit of treating as ultimate the proclamation of forgiveness through the work of the Messiah.

Sermon

Preachers should look for opportunities to reinforce the belief that all effective preaching and proclamation of the good news happens only through union with the Messiah who is the perfect prophet. Before the sermon, a prayer for illumination asks for the Holy Spirit to open ears and minds, to speak with power, and to transform those who hear. There are a few ways this prayer can connect with the peripatetic ministry of the Messiah to reinforce the habits of mission in union with him.

- Those who listened to Jesus often noticed that he preached with an authority they had not experienced elsewhere (Mark 1:22, 27; Matt

7:29). The prayer for illumination can appeal to this, reinforcing the habit of relying on the perfect prophetic work of Jesus Christ: "Lord Jesus Christ, you taught with authority on earth. Through the words we are about to hear, may you be the one teaching us through your Holy Spirit. As we proclaim the gospel, may we never rely on our eloquence, but only on your authority."

- Jesus also promised that his teaching authority would not disappear after he left his peripatetic ministry. He promised the Holy Spirit. A prayer based on this promise can also reinforce the habit of treating the proclamation of the gospel as ultimate: "Holy Spirit, our Lord Jesus promised that you would be with us to teach the world the gospel. May the good news be proclaimed here this morning, and may we never forget to proclaim the good news, relying on your promise to teach the world."

Sacraments

During his peripatetic ministry, Jesus often chastised the crowds for underestimating what he was up to. These texts can be used during the administration of the sacraments to reinforce the habit of relying on the perfect work of Jesus Christ. For example, the times when Jesus used miracles to feed multitudes and catch fish can be mentioned as a transition is made to between the meeting of physical needs represented by the elements on the table, and the meeting of spiritual needs that we believe happens through eating and drinking the body and blood of Jesus Christ. My own tradition's confession of faith provides a great summary of the meaning of the Supper along these lines ("Belgic Confession," Article 35). Explaining this relationship between physical needs and spiritual needs can help reinforce in us the habit of relying on the Messiah's perfect and spiritual work as we are engaged in so much of the ordinary, earthly work of our mission.

Prayers

Prayers can remind us that we pray in the name of the Messiah who does his perfect priestly work. During his peripatetic ministry, Jesus instructed us to pray in his name (John 15:16; 16:23). When we bring our petitions for the world during this season, we might end our prayers by saying, "We pray all this with confidence, because you told us to pray in your name. Amen."

Sending

As worshipers are sent out at the conclusion of worship, there will be opportunities to highlight the breadth of the Messiah's anointed work and the breadth of our work, in union with him. A charge can make this union explicit—reinforcing the habit of relying on the Messiah's perfect work. If the earlier portions of the liturgy or the sermon have focused on one particular aspect of the Messiah's threefold office or our work, the charge can be tailored to this:

- "Jesus Christ, our Prophet/Priest/King, sends you out to . . ." finishing with a description of the prophetic, priestly, or kingly work worshipers have been called to do.

The stories of Jesus' peripatetic ministry are easy to neglect in worship, but they show us something essential about Jesus Christ and our mission. They show us that Jesus Christ is the Messiah, anointed to do perfectly the work of a prophet, priest, and king. We need habits related to this as we are sent out into the world: imagining our mission as a broad thing, trusting the Messiah as the one whose work accomplishes the mission, and focusing on the proclamation of the good news as the ultimate piece of the mission. The season between Christmas and Lent is a great time to worship with liturgies like those above, as we depend on the Holy Spirit to teach us these habits of missional union with Christ, our Prophet, Priest, and King.

three

The Suffering, Crucifixion, and Death of Jesus

> Jesus replied, "The hour has come for the Son of Man to be glorified. Very truly I tell you, unless a kernel of wheat falls to the ground and dies, it remains only a single seed. But if it dies, it produces many seeds. Anyone who loves their life will lose it, while anyone who hates their life in this world will keep it for eternal life. Whoever serves me must follow me; and where I am, my servant also will be. My Father will honor the one who serves me." (John 12:23–26)

THOSE MIGHT BE SOME of the most terrifying words in the Gospel of John. Of course we want to be honored by the Father, right? Jesus tells us that honor is reserved for those who serve him. Of course we want to be the ones who serve Jesus, right? Jesus tells us that those who serve him are those who follow him. Of course we want to follow Jesus, right? Hold on! Jesus tells us that we have to follow him right as he sets out on the road to where? To the *cross!*? That's a road paved with humiliation, pain, and death. There will be an arrest. Whips will snatch blood from flesh. Nails will settle in between bone and muscle. Lungs, heart, and brain will fail. Jesus announces that he's turning down that road: "The hour has come for the Son of Man to be glorified." And then he says, "follow me." Those are terrifying words.

How exactly are we supposed to "follow" Jesus? At least some of us are, in fact, supposed to follow Jesus by surrendering our bodies and our lives for the purpose of his kingdom. A man named Ransom, a main character in C. S. Lewis's space trilogy, concludes in the second novel that this is his calling. He's found himself in a curious setting: a woman like Eve is being tempted by Satan. If she gives in, she will plunge her innocent planet into sin and evil. Ransom spends days and days arguing with this woman and Satan, trying to prevent another fall into sin. Eventually, Ransom understands: God the Son took on human flesh so that he could surrender it and conquer sin and evil on Earth. Ransom belongs to this flesh-and-blood surrendering Jesus Christ, and for him to follow Jesus in this setting is to surrender his body to stop the progress of sin. Ransom must not simply argue. He must fight, physically. And he will probably die. But he must follow Jesus. And a voice confirms it: "'It is not for nothing that you are named Ransom,' the Voice said. . . . 'My name also is Ransom,' said the Voice."[1] For Ransom to follow Jesus is to do what Jesus did: die for the sake of righteousness.

Some of us assume that to obey when Jesus says, "follow me," as he heads to the cross means nothing more than walking behind him at a distance and observing what happens. It's the same way we follow our children the first time they insist on using a public toilet by themselves, or the way we follow the news coming out of China. We keep our distance and observe. Is that what it means to "follow Jesus"? That is what some of Jesus' own disciples did as the events unfolded (Mark 14:50, 54; Luke 23:49), but it's not the kind of following Jesus expects. When he tells us to follow him, he wants us to do more than observe at a distance.

Is there some other way? Some kind of following between life-surrendering imitation and observation from a distance? There is. It's the way I'm confident Jesus wants most of us to follow him, and worship during the season of Lent can help teach us this way. But if worship during Lent is going to teach us this way, we who plan and lead worship might have to intentionally plan for it.

If you are involved in worship leadership, how do you plan for Lent? As each February approaches, I often find myself asking, "How soon should I start talking about the suffering and death of Jesus?" I don't remember observing Lent as a child. It's probable that my church ignored it. If anything, Lent was to me like the Perseid Meteor Shower: I was vaguely aware of its existence and that it occurred year after year; I knew some people were very interested in it; but I couldn't have told you anything about it myself. I probably wouldn't have noticed if I failed to observe both of them one year—Lent and the Perseid Meteor Shower.

---

1. Lewis, *Perelandra*, 125.

But now I'm a pastor, with the freedom to lead a church down a Lenten path. I plan out the course of my preaching. In our small church, I pick most of the songs we sing each week in worship. I get to tell the secretary whether the bulletin should label it "The First Sunday in Lent" or just "February 22" (or whatever it might be that year). And when I ask, "How should we observe Lent this year?" that question often means little more than "How soon should we start singing and talking about the suffering and death of Jesus?" It's the first Sunday of Lent. Should we sing "O Sacred Head, Now Wounded," "Alas! And Did My Savior Bleed," and "When I Survey the Wondrous Cross" yet, or should we wait awhile?

Lenten worship can be more than liturgically observing the death of Jesus. The hymnal we use, *Lift Up Your Hearts*, helpfully places these suffering-and-death hymns under the heading "Good Friday," suggesting we can save them for later in the season. We don't have to begin singing about Good Friday on the first Sunday of Lent. The texts in the Revised Common Lectionary focus on covenant, new life, and the cleansing waters of forgiveness.[2] Lent does not need to be "six-and-a-half weeks of marching around Mount Calvary."[3] Lenten liturgy can be about following Jesus some other way—this third way, something other than merely observing or actually dying for the kingdom.

This third way to follow Jesus is to be united to the Christ who suffered and died. Lent begins with Ash Wednesday, an opportunity "to meditate on our mortality, sinfulness, and need of a savior; to renew our commitment to daily repentance in the Lenten season and in all of life; and to remember with confidence and gratitude that Christ has conquered death and sin."[4] To follow Jesus is to be united to him—to be united to him so that we benefit from his suffering and dying and to be united to him so that we participate in his suffering and dying as we are sent out into the world. This union with a suffering Christ is something that liturgy can help us learn.

United to the Suffering Christ

In the way that Jesus means it, to follow him is to have union with him. It isn't a mere detached following-with-our-eyes to observe what happens to him. Nor is it always a straightforward following-with-our-bodies so that

2. Stookey, *Calendar*, 87–88.
3. Ibid., 88.
4. *Worship Sourcebook*, 547.

The Suffering, Crucifixion, and Death of Jesus

we suffer and die in a similar manner. To follow Jesus is to belong to him, to participate in him, to be united to him. What is true of him is in some way true of us.

So what is true of him? The Apostles' Creed summarizes the main events of his suffering: "He suffered under Pontius Pilate, was crucified, died, and was buried. He descended to hell." Each of these stages shows us something true about the person of Jesus. As he suffers under Pontius Pilate, we see his innocence. As he is crucified, we witness his willingness to suffer. As he dies, is buried, and descends to hell, we see the efficacy of his suffering. And in each of these, what is true of Jesus becomes true of us when we are united to him, when we "follow him."

He Suffered under Pontius Pilate Innocently

Jesus "suffered under Pontius Pilate." It seems that these words were included in the Apostles' Creed for the purpose of fixing the historicity of the crucifixion.[5] The suffering of Jesus Christ is not just a mythical account whose precise details are lost in the fog of time. No, Jesus suffered during the reign of a specific person—Pontius Pilate. This really happened in the history of this world. The words "under Pontius Pilate" affirm that. However, those words can mean something else, and this something else is critical for our understanding of union with Christ. John Calvin explained in his 1545 Geneva Catechism:

> He was justified by the testimony of the judge, to show that He did not suffer for His own unworthiness but for ours and yet He was solemnly condemned by the sentences of the same judge, to show that He is truly our surety, receiving condemnation for us in order to acquit us from it.[6]

The trial before Pontius Pilate was a necessary part of his suffering—and it is something that we need to know about. Something important would be missing if we didn't have that part of the accounts in the Gospels. Pontius Pilate confirmed that Jesus was innocent. After hearing the charges against Jesus and making his own inquiry into the matter, Pilate repeatedly delivered the same verdict: "I find no basis for a charge against him" (John 18:38; 19:4, 6). Against the background of acquittal, the sentencing

---

5. Klooster, *Our Only Comfort*, 480–82.
6. Calvin, "Calvin's Catechism (1545)," 476.

is especially stark: "Finally Pilate handed him over to them to be crucified" (John 19:16). Jesus uses Pontius Pilate's court to show the world that he suffered innocently.

Many others have suffered innocently. My wife was travelling in Italy with a friend recently, and while she was there I heard a podcast about an American woman who had been wrongly imprisoned in Italy. She had traveled there alone, apart from her family and community. She told of her difficulty trying to defend herself against murder charges in a foreign country. She recounted her relatives making trips to Italy to visit her in prison. I couldn't help but imagine that woman's story becoming, for me, something more than just a story on a podcast. What if my wife were arrested while on her trip, and her story began to approximate the story I was hearing on the podcast? What would it be like to make regular trips to Italy to visit her behind bars? But even if, somehow, the same thing would happen to my wife, at most their stories would run parallel to each other. Even if my wife were arrested, charged, and wrongly convicted of murder in Italy, her story would still only be *like* the story of the woman on the podcast. Their stories would never be the same story. With the innocent suffering of Jesus, however, things are different. If I put my faith in him, our stories converge. His story *is* my story. I am united to him, and because of this his innocent suffering belongs to me. I only *observe* that woman imprisoned in Italy, but I *follow* Jesus Christ.

His innocence is the foundation for my forgiveness. If he weren't innocent, he couldn't provide forgiveness. It would be like a man with a broken-down car offering to give you a ride. He'd be in no place to be offering a ride to someone else; he's got his own broken-down car. He ought to be asking for a ride. Similarly, if Jesus Christ had his own sins to pay for, his death could have done nothing more than pay for his sins. He couldn't have died for *my* sins. But he was innocent. His trial before Pontius Pilate confirms it. And to follow this innocent, suffering Christ is to be forgiven through confession, repentance, and faith. "If we confess our sins, he is faithful and just and will forgive us our sins." To follow Christ is to put the faith of forgiveness in him. Confession of sin, repentance, faith, being forgiven—this is what union with the innocent, suffering Christ means. This is what it is to follow Jesus as he suffers under Pontius Pilate.

Many pastors, no doubt, have counseled people who are overwhelmed with sorrow for their sins because they know that Jesus had to die for those very sins. They know they have done wrong, but that's not really what's eating them up. As they reflect on yesterday's transgression, they feel like they have crucified Jesus Christ all over again. That's what overwhelms them. We sing of this in a number of hymns:

> My Lord, what you did suffer was all for sinners' gain;
> Mine, mine was the transgression, but yours the deadly pain.
> So here I kneel, my Savior, for I deserve your place;
> Look on me with your favor and save me by your grace.
> (*O Sacred Head, Now Wounded,* translated by James W. Alexander)

> Was it for crimes that I have done
> He groaned upon the tree?
> . . .
> Thus might I hide my blushing face
> While his dear cross appears.
> (Isaac Watts, *Alas! And Did My Savior Bleed*)

Before he was tried by Pontius Pilate, found innocent, and brutally executed anyway, Jesus said, "follow me." He didn't mean that all of us would have to suffer wrongful execution for the sake of God's mission. But he also didn't mean that we should simply follow and watch, like Peter just inside the courtyard. Jesus suffered and died innocently. For us to follow our innocently suffering Christ is to confess our sins, put our trust in him, and be forgiven. For people who are torn up inside because their sins are the cause of Christ's crucifixion, union with Christ is the good news: because they follow him and are united to him, if they confess their sins, they are forgiven. His suffering is for them.

He Was Crucified Willingly

In the Apostles' Creed, we also say that Jesus "was crucified." There's something potentially misleading about saying it that way. It wasn't just that he "was crucified." The problem is the passive voice, but making it an active verb with Jesus as the object won't fix the problem: "His opponents crucified him." The problem is that all of this suggests that Jesus was passive in his crucifixion. He wasn't. Jesus' death was not something that just happened to him. Jesus *chose* crucifixion. Jesus was crucified willingly, and his willingness explains a certain curiosity about Christianity: crosses adorn our necks, our Bibles, our church furniture, our steeples, our walls, our art, our everything. The cross is the central image of Christianity. But the cross is the thing that killed our Savior! Why would we Christians use as our central symbol the object that was used to kill Jesus Christ? It would be unthinkable for other devotees to do the same. I hesitate to offer examples, because they sound so offensive. But that's actually the point. Imagine the fans of Princess Diana adorning themselves with smashed-automobile jewelry, or a foundation devoted to the legacy of Martin Luther King Jr. using stationery with the image of a pistol on it. Those are revolting ideas, and yet, it seems that this is what Christians do every day: we lift high the cross! But we do this for a good reason. We do this because of the willingness of Jesus Christ. He chose the cross, so we choose it as our emblem. The cross that we see prominently displayed during the season of Lent should remind us of the willingness of Jesus Christ.

The willingness of Jesus to be crucified can be on display a number of times during the Lenten season. Consider Palm Sunday. It seems like such a cheery event—the crowds acclaiming Jesus as their king. In fact, it is so cheery that some have worried about congregations being *too* cheerful on Palm Sunday—we need to make sure we notice the darkness of the season.[7] Only by wearing the most tightly-fitted blinders can a worshiper make it through Palm Sunday worship without confronting the grave irony of the day. Jesus surely knew what we know as we worship: that we're going to be returning here for worship on Good Friday! The Triumphal Entry was only "triumphal" in the most macabre sense. And Jesus surely knew.

Matthew, the Gospel writer, knew the significance of mounting that donkey to ride into Jerusalem, writing that it fulfilled a prophecy from the Old Testament prophet Zechariah: "Say to Daughter Zion, 'See, your king comes to you, gentle and riding on a donkey, and on a colt, the foal of a donkey'" (Matt 21:4–5). That's not just a description of a king. That's a description of a humble king, a "gentle" king, as Zechariah put it. After all, what kind of king would ride into his city on a *donkey*? Only a humble, meek king.[8] Jesus willingly rode in on that donkey as Zechariah prophesied, not only proclaiming himself to be the king we so joyfully celebrate on Palm Sunday. He also proclaimed himself to be Zechariah's *humble* king, humility that will reach its depths on the cross later in the week. Later in the week, he said to Judas Iscariot: "What you are about to do, do quickly" (John 13:27). It sounds like Jesus is giving Judas permission to betray him.

---

7. *Worship Sourcebook*, 587–88.
8. Sherman, *King, Priest, and Prophet*, 122–23, 145–47.

The Suffering, Crucifixion, and Death of Jesus

That's how the other disciples understood it. They didn't understand what the instruction was about (John 13:29), but they understood that Jesus was giving permission. Jesus willingly let Judas betray him. Later, in the Garden of Gethsemane, he prayed: "Father, if you are willing, take this cup from me; yet not my will, but yours be done" (Luke 22:42). Jesus surrendered the impulses of his human will to the divine will. He willingly was crucified.

So, what does it mean to have union with this willingly crucified Christ? When we witness the willful generosity of people we love we respond with active gratitude. Being united to a willingly crucified Jesus should evoke a similar response: active gratitude.

A total solar eclipse crossed the United States in August 2017, and my family witnessed it while visiting a relative of a relative in Tennessee. About a month before the visit, I noticed that this couple lived directly in the path of totality, and I emailed asking if they just had room for us to pitch a tent in their yard the night before the eclipse. I suppose we invited ourselves over. I figured that if that was a social error, it would be forgivable, but it was not the last social error we committed. Our hosts were generous and hospitable. They would not allow us to sleep outside. They willingly cleared out beds in their home for us and our two children, even though they had other visitors for the event. As we pulled in their driveway, we realized we were about to commit a second error: we had not brought any kind of gift for our hosts. And we did worse. Our hosts were also generous and hospitable for meals. They insisted on preparing dinner, breakfast, and lunch for us. As we sat down to eat dinner the evening we arrived, and our hosts were bringing out the pulled pork, we inadvertently revealed that we usually eat a vegetarian diet. We had planned to keep that quiet, eating what was served in quantities that would be both polite and which we would be comfortable eating. But things don't always work out as planned, and our hosts found out about our diet. Immediately, they were substituting ingredients and changing breakfast plans for the next morning—continuing to offer their generous hospitality. Our hosts kept willingly offering their generosity as we continued to commit social errors. They opened their home and their cupboards. They allowed us to inconvenience them even in the course of the meals.

So, what is the right way to respond? A person might theoretically respond by taking advantage of them, thinking, "I'm going to return here. It was like a free bed and breakfast. How could I turn down such great service at no cost?" However, they were so willingly generous that a response like that is impossible. The only appropriate response is active gratitude—looking for ways to show them thanks in the future.

Union with a willingly crucified Christ inspires a similar gratitude. When you know that Christ was crucified willingly, you can't possibly respond in any other way than with acts of gratitude. This point is always made when the doctrine of free grace is challenged: *if God freely offers forgiveness, why wouldn't Christians simply continue in sin?* The apostle Paul wrote about this question: "What shall we say, then? Shall we go on sinning so that grace may increase? By no means! . . . What then? Shall we sin because we are not under law but under grace? By no means!" (Rom 6:1–2, 15). During the Reformation, churches frequently had to answer the same question, as they emphasized justification by grace alone through faith, and not by works. "Won't this doctrine lead to carelessness in doing good works?" *That's impossible!* is the continual answer.[9]

If you look closely at the ways Paul and the church have responded to this question, you'll see that gratitude is not simply the result of *knowing* that Christ was willingly crucified. Acts of gratitude result from a deeper spiritual union with this willingly crucified Christ. Paul describes this gratitude-producing union as a matter of life (Rom 6:4), a transfer to servitude to a new master (Rom 6:18), and, importantly, as a matter of having a mind controlled by the Spirit of Christ (Rom 8:1–17). Christ was willingly crucified, willingly obedient. If you are united to him, you have his Spirit working in you, making you willingly obedient. To be united to a willingly crucified Christ is to be willingly obedient to God in thankfulness yourself.

He Died, Was Buried, and Descended to Hell Efficaciously

Finally, Jesus "died, was buried, and descended to hell." The line in the Creed about the descent to hell is terribly controversial,[10] and we aren't going to sort through the controversy here. Note, however, the standard Presbyterian understanding of these three clauses: "Christ's humiliation after His death consisted in His being buried, and continuing in the state of the dead, and under the power of death till the third day, which hath been otherwise expressed in these words: 'He descended into hell.'"[11] According

---

9. For example, "Belgic Confession," Article 24; "Heidelberg Catechism," Q&A 64.

10. For a summary of the debate from a confessional Reformed perspective, see Hyde, "In Defense of *Descendit*," 104–17.

11. "Larger Catechism," Q&A 50.

to this understanding, all three of these clauses mean the same thing: Jesus really died a real human death. There are good reasons to say this three times. One reason is that we might mistakenly imagine that Jesus, as God himself, is only somewhat like a human. To remember that our God, God the Son, took on mortality and really died, we say "he died" three different ways: "He died, he was buried, he descended to hell." He really died because he is a real human being. However, there is another reason to say this three times: to emphasize that something important and world-changing happened in his death. Consider the Heidelberg Catechism: "Why does the creed add 'He descended to hell'? To assure me during attacks of deepest great and temptation that Christ my Lord, by suffering unspeakable anguish, pain, and terror of soul, on the cross but also earlier, has delivered me from hellish anguish and torment."[12] He died, he was buried, and he descended to hell. This all means that his death was effective. It really accomplished something. He died efficaciously.

We often repeat important news to indicate that the event is really important; it means something; it effects a new reality. On September 11, 2001, I heard the words: "They're flying planes into the World Trade Center and the Pentagon!" I chuckled. It wasn't because I thought a horrific terrorist attack was funny. Not at all. I couldn't comprehend the world-changing nature of the news. *The person must be talking about some video game or movie or something*, I thought. *That can't really be happening.* "No, this is real. The World Trade Center and the Pentagon have been hit with planes." Then my mind was filled with questions: *What do you mean? Why would someone do that? Who is doing that?* Finally, I rounded the corner into a room with a television and saw the images. And that's when I heard the host explain: "Three airliners have struck the World Trade Center and the Pentagon." When I heard the news the third time, I began to understand the significance. This was not some accident. This isn't some statement that you can chortle away, saying, *Hmm, imagine that.* This changes everything.

Saying "he died, was buried, and he descended to hell" is like that. Those words all may point to a similar reality—the real human mortality of Jesus Christ in body and soul. When we say it that many ways, however, we signify the efficacy. He died, and it accomplished something. It accomplished everything. In his death, he put to death all sin and evil. He died triumphantly. He died once-for-all. He died efficaciously. Missiologist Christopher Wright describes the mission of God at the cross:

12. "Heidelberg Catechism," Q&A 44.

God's mission was that:

- sin should be punished and sinners forgiven.
- evil should be defeated and humanity liberated.
- death should be destroyed and life and immortality brought to light
- enemies should be reconciled to one another and to God.
- creation itself should be restored and reconciled to its creator.[13]

Jesus Christ died efficaciously and accomplished all of this.

What then does it mean to be united to him? Go through each of those lines from Wright and place yourself in it. You leave with the confidence of a series of "no mores." No more condemnation (Rom 3:21): to be united to a Christ who died efficaciously is to have the punishment for your sins meted out and to be forgiven. No more evil powers (Col 2:14): when you belong to Christ, you don't fear the forces of evil that attack you every day. You know that you are allied with the one who has already won the decisive victory over them. No more death (Heb 2:14): are you united to Christ? Then death is destroyed. This doesn't mean that you won't die. You will, unless Jesus returns before some injury or disease does you in. But if you belong to Jesus, that death doesn't have *final* power over you. Death, for you, is not your eternal fate. Death is the doorway to eternal life. No more division (Eph 2:14–16): the death of Jesus Christ effects the reconciliation between enemies and with God. If you are united to Jesus Christ, you are reconciled with your enemies in him, and, even better, you are reconciled with God. Finally, no more yearning (Col 1:20): to be united to the Christ who died efficaciously is to belong to a creation that will be restored. Through union with Christ who suffered efficaciously, you go through life with the hope and confidence that there will be no more of any of that.

When we follow Jesus to the cross, especially during the season of Lent, this doesn't mean that we merely watch from a distance and see what happens. It's not like following a news story or a sports team. To follow Jesus is to be united to him—to the one who suffered innocently, who was crucified willingly, and who died efficaciously—in confession, in grateful living, and in confident hope. The *Worship Sourcebook* sums this up nicely in its description of Ash Wednesday: "The aim of Ash Wednesday worship is threefold: to meditate on our mortality, sinfulness, and need of a savior; to renew our commitment to daily repentance in the Lenten season and in

---

13. Wright, *Mission of God*, 313–14.

all of life; and to remember with confidence and gratitude that Christ has conquered death and sin."[14]

Mission in Union with the Suffering Christ

When I was about sixteen years old, I was waterskiing one Saturday afternoon. As the boat pulled me near the beach where some of my family was sitting, I let go of the rope and began to coast in toward shore. I waited for the moment when my speed would no longer keep me on top of the water, and I would sink. I planned on pulling off my skis and swimming with them to shore. That's not what happened. As the sand rapidly approached, I realized I wasn't going to sink. I was coming in too fast. Before I had time to think about it, my skis hit the sand in three inches of water and came to a complete stop. My body did not come to a complete stop. I thought for sure I was going to look like a fool or even be injured, thrown out of my skis face-first onto the beach. Instead, it was fantastic. Yes, my body kept moving forward as my skis came to a complete stop. But my feet popped out of the boots, and I immediately found my balance. Without slowing I continued jogging up the beach. One second I was skiing; the next I was jogging as though I had planned the whole thing.

I often thought about attempting the same thing again. Performing that maneuver intentionally would require a precise intuition of how my relationship with the boat affected my speed coming into shore. I could come into shore at different speeds by skiing with the boat's direction of travel or across the boat's direction of travel just before I let go of the rope, and I would need to be able to control that very carefully as I evaluated the distance to shore. The key dynamic would be this: the way I followed the boat would in every way affect the way I approached the shore. (I never tried it. I really didn't want to end up face-first in the sand.)

A similar dynamic, however, holds for following a suffering Christ. Just as how a skier follows a boat affects how the skier approaches other objects, how we follow Jesus Christ affects how we approach everyone else in the world. Union with an innocent, willing, and efficaciously suffering Christ is not just about our personal salvation. That union is not just about forgiveness, gratitude, and hope. It is about our God-given mission—our approach to the world.

---

14. *Worship Sourcebook*, 547.

Worship, Mission, and the Church Year

Mission in Union with an Innocent Christ

We follow a Savior who suffered innocently in our place. We belong to the one who was acquitted, yet punished because of our sins. This is a blessing for us—we're forgiven—but it should also be a blessing to others. Because we follow a Savior who suffered innocently in our place, we approach others with humility and grace. We should ask humble and contrite Lenten questions like the ones Laurence Hull Stookey suggests: "What attitudes do I convey to those who irritate me? How can awareness of my own need of God's grace enable me to be more gracious to them?"[15] We should ask others for forgiveness. If we are united to a Savior who suffered innocently for our sake, if his cruel execution was what our crimes deserve, then we ought to force three little words out of our mouths time and time again: "Will you forgive me?"

It's hard to force those words out, sometimes. I've struggled with this. I vividly remember sitting in the leather chair in my office and wrestling with the pride that keeps those words bottled up, grasping for the humility that would produce those words. I seethed over how the other person had wronged me. I analyzed their sins. I detailed how they should have acted and what they should have said. I fantasized about the words I could use to demand an apology from them. Then, I heard the suggestion of the Holy Spirit: "Perhaps you should ask for their forgiveness." I batted away the thought as quickly as it arose. "Perhaps I should ask for their forgiveness," came the thought again. *But I can't do that. I absolutely refuse! The other person is much more at fault than I.* "Perhaps I should ask for their forgiveness." Perhaps I should. After all, I need forgiveness so badly that Jesus Christ had to suffer a brutal execution in my place. I belong to him, the one who suffered innocently for me. And if I belong to him, I should be asking for forgiveness. I spoke those words from the heart: "I should not have said what I said. I should not have done what I did. I am sorry. Will you please forgive me?"

Craig Van Gelder and Dwight Zscheile identify 2 Corinthians 5 as a key text that links Christ's innocent suffering with our mission to pursue reconciliation:

> God was reconciling the world to himself in Christ, not counting people's sins against them. And he has committed to us the message of reconciliation. We are therefore Christ's ambassadors,

---

15. Stookey, *Calendar*, 82.

The Suffering, Crucifixion, and Death of Jesus

> as though God were making his appeal through us. We implore you on Christ's behalf: Be reconciled to God. God made him who had no sin to be sin for us, so that in him we might become the righteousness of God. (2 Cor 5:19–21)[16]

The mission of reconciliation that Paul writes of there is the mission of calling people to be reconciled to God through faith in Jesus Christ. For that, however, we must be humble—humble enough to ask for forgiveness. Michael Frost tells the story of two Christian families who helped their neighborhood in Edmonton, Canada learn humility. One family in the neighborhood had a son who was involved with a gang. Twice, rival gang members drove through this quiet community and shot up the house to warn this son. The other neighbors began murmuring and devising ways to make the family move. The two Christian families, however, managed to convince the neighbors to change their approach, humbling themselves before the terrorized family, seeking forgiveness and reconciliation with them in order to stand with them in their struggle. Those families engaged in their God-given mission in union with a Savior who suffered innocently. If you are united with him, you go out in the world humbly confessing even to others your sins for which your Savior suffered on your behalf.

Mission in Union with a Willing Christ

As we engage in our God-given mission, we also follow a Savior who was crucified willingly. As explained above, this willingness of Christ is inspiring. It's inspiring in the ordinary way we use that word: I think about his willingness to die; I'm *inspired* to respond in gratitude. The willingness of Christ is also *in-spiring* in a more literal way: The *Spirit* is *in* me. The Holy Spirit of the willing Christ is in me and makes me share in his willingness. All this inspiration applies just as much to my own spiritual growth as it does to my interaction with others, my God-given mission to the world.

Sometimes we ignore that second part. Sometimes we imagine that living in thankfulness to God involves only our own self-improvement. Jesus calls us to "take up our crosses." He tells us that following him means being willing to lose our own lives for the sake of our calling (Matt 16:24–25). That sounds harsh, but there's an easy way out: imagine that the life you must be willing to lose is nothing more than the "old self" that is crucified

---

16. Van Gelder and Zschiele, *Missional Church in Perspective*, 117.

with Christ (Rom 6:1–11). This is a low-risk way to follow Jesus. It's hardly a loss to give up my old way of life, when that means giving up something shameful so that I can be raised to something honorable. I'm giving up a bad version of myself so that I can gain a good version, right? It might be painful and difficult at the time. But in the end, I'll be a better person. If that's all that it means to "take up our crosses," then we've found an easy way out.

Michael Frost calls the person who assumes this a "pietist." The pietist is a Christian who is driven by a desire to live a holy, God-pleasing life and a fear that unbelievers around them will corrupt them. They try to please God more and more by their inward holiness. Trying to please God is, in itself, not wrong. We should want our lives to be "holy and pleasing to God" (Rom 12:1). But if that's all we want, we're being lazy and selfish, Frost argues.[17] We're looking for an easy way to follow Jesus, one that brings us into minimal contact with others.

To follow a Christ who willingly suffered is to be willing in your own way. You take up your cross not just with respect to your old self but also with respect to others. You will willingly give up not only who you used to be, but you'll also willingly give up things that are valuable to you even now. You'll do this for the sake of others. Mission in union with a willing Christ is not just about self-improvement, it is about self-sacrifice for the sake of others. That's what you'll do if you really are *inspired* to acts of gratitude by the willingness of Jesus Christ to be crucified.

Mission in Union with an Efficacious Christ

The efficacy of Christ's death also has everything to do with our God-given mission. Union with a Christ whose death really accomplished something gives us hope. Don't keep that hope to yourself. That hope is for the world and the people around you, too. Hope is not just for comfort. Hope is for action and for witness.

Lois Barrett and others studied twelve churches that exhibited some missional characteristics, and they noticed some patterns among these churches. One of the patterns was risk-taking. These missional churches engaged in nonviolent resistance, self-sacrifice, and counter-cultural living. None of this was safe.[18] All of it is based on hope. Christopher Wright

17. Frost, *The Road to Missional*, 84–86.
18. Barrett, "Taking Risks," 74–83.

describes why missional risk-taking is based on hope: "On what basis dare we challenge the chains of Satan, in word and deed, in people's spiritual, moral, physical, and social lives? Only through the cross."[19] Wright goes on to describe the things that the cross accomplished: forgiveness, the defeat of evil, the destruction of death, reconciliation between enemies, and the restoration of creation. He writes, "every dimension of that good news is good news utterly and only because of the blood of Christ on the cross."[20] We have hope for those areas of life, hope that motivates us to take risks in those areas, because Christ's death was efficacious.

Think about your own church or your own family. What risks might God be calling you to take as part of your mission? But more importantly: why aren't you taking them? And most importantly: what would make you more inclined to take those missional risks? Let me suggest an answer to that third question: Union with a Christ who died efficaciously would prompt you to take those risks. Paul wrote about the effects of hope as he contemplated his own uncertain future:

> I eagerly expect and hope that I will in no way be ashamed, but will have sufficient courage so that now as always Christ will be exalted in my body, whether by life or by death. For to me, to live is Christ and to die is gain. If I am to go on living in the body, this will mean fruitful labor for me. Yet what shall I choose? I do not know! I am torn between the two: I desire to depart and be with Christ, which is better by far; but it is more necessary for you that I remain in the body. Convinced of this, I know that I will remain, and I will continue with all of you for your progress and joy in the faith, so that through my being with you again your boasting in Christ Jesus will abound on account of me. (Phil 1:20–26)

Paul didn't know exactly what would become of his life. But he did know that Jesus Christ's death accomplished something for him—it secured eternal life for him. Christ died efficaciously; death would not be his end. With that hope, Paul could engage in the work more boldly. Perhaps his further work would involve chains and more imprisonment. Perhaps his further work would involve dying a martyr's death. Ultimately, none of that mattered. Jesus Christ had died, and his death secured Paul's own future. Hope leads to risk-taking and hard work. That was true for Paul, and it is true for you.

---

19. Wright, *Mission of God*, 315.
20. Ibid., 315.

Hope is also for others. Giving other people real hope is one of the things that brings me the most joy. A few years ago, I considered an opportunity that would have taken me out of pastoral ministry. I decided not to pursue it, and hope was one of the decisive considerations. I have so many opportunities to give hope to others as a pastor. I thought specifically about the funerals I would not be doing if I were no longer a pastor. I couldn't give that up. I love giving people hope when they need it the most. You don't have to be a pastor to give people hope, however. (With that realization, perhaps I should go back and reconsider that other opportunity!) In fact, the Bible makes it clear that you *must* give people hope even if you're not a pastor. Sharing hope is your God-given mission: ". . . and so we will be with the Lord forever. Therefore encourage each other with these words" (1 Thess 4:17b–18). Comfort each other with words of hope. This is part of what it means to engage in your God-given mission as you follow a Christ who died efficaciously. His death firmly establishes that hope. Share it with others.

Missional Liturgy for Lent

I hope that you've been thinking, "I've got to do a better job at some of this." If you've been taking this seriously, you'll have noticed that you need to do better. Look around: your fellow believers need to do a better job, too. We all need to learn the habits of union with Christ better. Worship can be part of this, especially worship during Lent, when we have a perfect opportunity to worship in union with a Christ who suffered innocently, who was crucified willingly, and who died efficaciously.

Liturgy for Union with an Innocently Suffering Christ

This year, on the first Sunday of Lent, our congregation did something different: we confessed our sins aloud together. Don't worry, I didn't ask people to name their own particular sins aloud. Instead, we prayed this prayer together:

> Most merciful God, whose Son, Jesus Christ, was tempted in every way, yet was without sin, we confess our sins before you. We admit our failures before the whole world. We have not lived righteously. Our hands have not been clean. We have lashed out in anger. We have followed the lusts of our hearts. We have turned from your

decrees. We have not been blameless before you. Forgive us, in the
name of Jesus and by the righteousness of Jesus. Amen.

This prayer helped us to practice mission in union with an innocently suffering Christ in two ways. First, the content of the prayer aimed us in the right direction. We professed the sinlessness of Jesus Christ, and then we confessed—before the world, no less—our own contrasting sinfulness. This contrast between our blame and Christ's blamelessness continued as we appealed to the righteousness of Christ for our forgiveness. Just saying the words of a prayer like this can help us learn the practice of acknowledging our sinfulness in contrast to Christ's innocence. A second feature of this prayer also helped us to learn this habit: we said the prayer aloud together. Many congregations read litanies together in worship. Worshipers in these churches are used to picking up the bulletin or looking at the screen and praying a prayer in unison. We don't do that very often in our church. Maybe this made the practice more memorable, more formative. I don't know. But it is perfectly suited for mission in union with an innocently suffering Christ. Why? In the prayer, we *said*, "We admit our failures before the world," but to actually say the prayer aloud is to practice that. We all said, so that our neighbors could hear: "We have lashed out in anger. We have followed the lusts of our hearts." (Those were themes that would come up later in the sermon on Matthew 5:21–30.) In that small way, we practiced being humble before the world.

Other liturgies can help worshipers practice missional union with an innocently suffering Christ. Prayers of confession can use the first-person singular: "*I* have hated my neighbor." Prayers of confession can be honest about the congregation's failings: "We have failed to give as generously as we could have to help those suffering this recent natural disaster." The point is that the petitions can be particularized,[21] either to ourselves or to specific sins. This helps worshipers learn to see themselves in the world as sinners united to a sinless Christ. Pastor Mike Cosper is convinced that pointed prayers of confession are an important part of being hospitable to visitors.[22] What a great witness to visitors when a congregation doesn't pretend to be a perfect place of smiles and sacredness and instead just openly admits that they've failed! When worshipers do this in worship, perhaps even aware of the visitors who are there with them hearing these things, they'll learn the habit of heading out into the world, on their God-given missions, as

---

21. Schmit, *Sent and Gathered*, 170.
22. Cosper, *Rhythms of Grace*, 130–31.

humble people. They'll learn the habit of missional union with an innocently suffering Jesus Christ.

Liturgy for Union with a Willingly Crucified Christ

Liturgies can help worshipers also learn the habit of taking up their crosses in gratitude as they follow a Christ who was willingly crucified. One of our denomination's traditional prayers for after the celebration of the Lord's Supper teaches this attitude: "Enable us henceforth to live always for him who gave himself for us, even our Lord Jesus Christ . . . ."[23] Maybe the best place in worship, however, to practice missional union with a willingly crucified Christ is the offering. On the third Sunday of Lent, our congregation took up an offering for the church-planting efforts of our denomination. Typically, the offering would be introduced with a basic explanation of what it was for: "The offering is for Christian Reformed Home Missions." This Sunday, however, the liturgy before the offering and the sermon that followed emphasized the faithfulness of Jesus Christ to his promise and his role as our Savior. It was a perfect Sunday to focus on the willingness of Jesus Christ as he was crucified, and it was a perfect Sunday for the liturgy to help worshipers learn some of the habits of willingly taking up their crosses in gratitude. The offering was introduced this way, using the same word, "faithfulness," that was repeatedly used to describe Jesus Christ's willingness to be crucified: "We've pledged ourselves to God's mission. Let's practice faithfulness to that pledge . . . ." In this small way, we practiced following a willingly crucified Christ with our own willingness to give up what is precious to us for the sake of our God-given mission. That Communion prayer and the words spoken to introduce the offering are small things, but habits are taught through the accumulation of many small things.

Liturgy for Union with a Christ Who Died Efficaciously

The efficacy of Christ's death ought to change how we pursue our God-given mission out in the world. We need to learn how to engage in this mission in union with a Christ whose death accomplished so much. Liturgy can help us learn this, too.

---

23. *Psalter Hymnal*, 982.

The Suffering, Crucifixion, and Death of Jesus

Naming stark realities in worship is one of the best ways to learn this habit through liturgy. On two other Lenten Sundays in our congregation, worship centered around the theme of the efficacy of Christ's death. One Sunday, when the sermon was from Matthew 6:1–18, we noticed how Jesus died to put to death our prideful, boastful, arrogant selves. "For we know that our old self was crucified with him so that the body of sin might be done away with," Paul writes in Romans 6. This reality needs to empower more than our own personal sanctification. This reality needs to give us confidence as we head out into a world cruelly spoiled by all sorts of prideful, boastful, arrogant people. In our liturgy, we named all of that ugliness, practicing the habit of confidence that our own contributions to this kind of evil are put to death through the death of Jesus. To do this, we read Psalm 131 together:

> My heart is not proud, O Lord,
>   my eyes are not haughty;
> I do not concern myself with great matters
>   or things too wonderful for me.
> But I have stilled and quieted my soul;
>   like a weaned child with its mother,
>   like a weaned child is my soul within me.
> O Israel, put your hope in the Lord
>   both now and forevermore.

Stark realities are especially important in prayers of lament. Not every congregation is accustomed to praying this way, but lament is an excellent way to connect the harsh realities of the world to the completed work of Jesus Christ. That's why Cosper recommends it.[24] For congregations that are unaccustomed to lament, praying whole psalms of lament is a good place to start. The pastor, elder, or worship leader who usually offers intercessory prayers should also get acquainted with the kind of language used in these psalms. Start sprinkling *Why, O Lord?* into the prayers now and then. The language can feel awkward, because we seem to be complaining to God. The Psalms show us, however, that these prayers are appropriate when we voice our laments and then appeal to the grace and mercy of God.

In fact, every time a congregation prays to God for something, that prayer should be followed up with an appeal to what Jesus Christ has accomplished. When our prayers appeal to what Jesus Christ has effected in

---

24. Cosper, *Rhythms of Grace*, 135.

his death, not just in lament but in confession and intercession as well, we learn the habit of going out into the world as people who are united to a Christ who has accomplished redemption once for all. Mike Cosper makes this point about assuring the congregation that their sins are forgiven: we need to make sure we never forget where the good news comes from. It comes from Christ's atoning work.[25] Lent is an ideal time for these appeals to be made to the effective death of Jesus Christ. For example, after praying about those who have suffered an act of war or for restraint for nations that are threatening hostilities, the worship leader can say this: "We confess together, O God: Jesus Christ died, and with him he took death to the grave. Through this, give the hope of life to a world gripped by the fear of more death, more war."

Theologian Mark Labberton describes many other ways liturgy confronts the powers of the world. For example, a call to worship acknowledges God's ultimate power, prayers of adoration lift up the one true God, prayers of confession appeal to the one who has the power to forgive, and baptism acknowledges that God has claimed us amid all the powers that try to put their mark on us. In all of this and more, worship confronts the powers of the world that demand our allegiance. The completed work of Jesus Christ is the only reason we can do all of this in worship.[26] He is Lord. His lordship is established in his death, as he "disarmed the powers and authorities" (Col 2:15). The act of worship itself, and so many of the liturgies we use in worship, teach us the habit of going out into the world as people who follow a Christ who died efficaciously. His death accomplished it. That's why we have missional confidence.

When Jesus says, "follow me," we're tempted to ignore the words because they are too demanding, or we're tempted to domesticate the words and act like they mean very little. Following Jesus, however, is first of all a matter of being united to him. Following Jesus—the Christ who suffered, was crucified, and died—is a matter of being forgiven, of being inspired to gratitude, and of having confidence that redemption has been accomplished. All of this must be lived out in the way we pursue our God-given mission. It should be obvious from the way we humbly confess to others that we follow a Christ who suffered innocently. People should be able to see from the way we willingly surrender what is precious to us that we follow a Christ who willingly was crucified for us. Our confidence should be

---

25. Cosper, *Rhythms of Grace*, 138.
26. Labberton, *Dangerous Act*, 109–31.

noticeable—because our confidence comes from the fact that we follow a Christ who accomplished so much in his death. These things need to be habits for us, and we can learn these habits through the liturgies we use in Lenten worship.

four

The Resurrection of Jesus

One Easter Sunday, I asked some first-generation immigrants how to say "Happy Easter" in Dutch. I was surprised by the answers. I guess there are a few different ways to say it— "Eastertime," "Easter festival," or "Easter day." The people I asked didn't agree, but that wasn't what surprised me. Instead, I was surprised to hear that each of the Dutch words for "Easter" began with *paas*—*Paasdag, Paasfeest,* and so on. We have a similar Easter-related word in English—"paschal." It's a variation of the Hebrew word for Passover, and it is rarely heard outside seminary classrooms. Apparently, things are different in the Netherlands. That sound—*paas*—which connects the resurrection and the Passover, is an everyday word. I guess I shouldn't have been surprised. It turns out that this is the case in many languages. Theologian Laurence Hull Stookey half-heartedly wished that we in the English-speaking world could start using the term "Pasch" instead of "Easter." Can you imagine this? English-speaking congregations everywhere being greeted with "Blessed Pasch" on Easter Sunday? Even Stookey admitted that's probably not going to happen.[1] I wonder whether I might be able to get away with it in my congregation where the vast majority have Dutch ancestry, and many are first-generation immigrants....

It would be good to start calling the holiday "Pasch" because that term connects the celebration of the resurrection with Passover. Good Friday and Easter occur near the Jewish Passover, as they did the year of Jesus' death and resurrection. Even more importantly, the resurrection of Jesus Christ is the fulfillment of the Old Testament Passover. Easter Sunday is about the eternal exodus. Easter Sunday is about deliverance.

---

1. Stookey, *Calendar,* 53–54.

When we are sent out into the world by God, we see the need for deliverance all around us. Every time we see this need for deliverance, we see a need for the risen Jesus Christ. We see ourselves trapped in shame and guilt; we need to be delivered. We see ourselves run ragged because we're trying to serve all the masters in our lives; we need to be delivered. We see ourselves subjected to all kinds of physical pain and suffering because of human oppressors and medical problems; we need to be delivered. We need an exodus. Our world needs the risen Jesus Christ.

God sends us, his church, out into a world that needs the risen Jesus Christ, and he expects us to play some role in helping the world come to find its deliverance in him. How can we get ready for that role? How can we be prepared to do our part? True Christian worship is union with Christ that can form us for mission. Easter and the resurrection are about deliverance, and worship is in union with Christ. Because of that, we can expect Easter worship to shape us for that mission of deliverance. When we worship at Easter, we are united to Jesus Christ as the one who is risen from the dead. How does this union with the risen Jesus Christ shape us for mission, and what liturgies are especially appropriate for this union? Before answering these questions, let's simply consider what it means to be united to the resurrected Jesus Christ for us and our salvation.

United with the Risen Christ

To be united to the resurrected Jesus Christ is to be delivered, and deliverance is an essential part of God's mission in the Bible. We see this in the exodus from Egypt. The books of Genesis and Exodus tell us the story: Jacob's family had traveled to Egypt to escape a famine in the land of Canaan. They settled in Egypt. Over many generations, the family became a large ethnic group, and they were subjected to increasing oppression by the Egyptians. Finally, God acted through Moses to deliver them from Egypt, the land of slavery. God wasn't just helping the Israelites emigrate. The exodus was deliverance in a number of different dimensions—because God's deliverance is always multi-dimensional. It's helpful to boil down those dimensions of deliverance to three: God delivers the Israelites so that they can put justifying faith in him, so that they can worship and serve him, and so that their bodies can be free. These correspond to the three benefits of the resurrection that Calvin identified in his Geneva Catechism,[2] and which are reflected in Question and Answer 45 of the Heidelberg Catechism:

> How does Christ's resurrection benefit us?
> First, by his resurrection he has overcome death, so that he might make us share in the righteousness he obtained for us by his death.
> Second, by his power we too are already raised to a new life.
> Third, Christ's resurrection is a sure pledge to us of our blessed resurrection.[3]

These three—righteousness by faith, transformation for service, and the resurrection of the body—are three main dimensions of what it means to be united to a resurrected Jesus Christ.

Righteousness by Faith

Centuries before the exodus, God delivered Abram from doubt. God had promised that his descendants would become a great nation, but Abram had a seemingly good reason to be skeptical: he had no children. God reiterated his promise, and we read that "Abram believed the LORD, and he credited it to him as righteousness" (Gen 15:6). God delivered Abram from doubting, bringing him to the righteousness that comes only by faith. The enslaved Israelites in Egypt might have needed a similar deliverance. It's easy to imagine the difficulty of putting faith in God while living as an Israelite in Egypt. There were all sorts of reasons to doubt God. The influential Nile River and the omnipresent sun were regarded as gods by the Egyptians. Divinity was supposedly found in powerful Pharaoh, and his royal magicians were thought to have supernatural power. God delivered the Israelites from all of this. In the plagues that preceded the Passover, God revealed himself as the one true God over the false gods.[4] He revealed himself as the only true supernatural power as the magicians were progressively unable to replicate God's wonders through Moses. God delivered the Israelites from a climate of confusion and doubt in Egypt to the righteousness that comes only through faith in him.

---

2. Calvin, "Calvin's Catechism (1545)," 478–79.
3. "Heidelberg Catechism," Q&A 45.
4. Wright, *Mission of God*, 270–71.

The Resurrection of Jesus

The resurrection of Jesus includes a similar deliverance for us: in the resurrection, Jesus is revealed to us for our faith as our only Savior.[5] Through faith in this risen Savior, we are justified, counted righteous before God. It would be impossible for us to have justifying faith in Jesus Christ if he had not risen from the dead. That is at least part of what Paul means when he writes that Jesus "was raised to life for our justification" (Rom 4:25).

As the keystone event in the life and work of Jesus, the resurrection benefits us in many ways. This chapter only scratches the surface, even with the discussion of new life and a bodily resurrection below. However, at least one benefit of the resurrection is that our knowledge of it enables us to put saving faith in Jesus. The resurrection proves to us that our sins have been completely forgiven in Christ. Can you imagine having faith in Jesus Christ as the one who fully paid for your sins, if his body had remained in the tomb?

Maybe you can. It is, after all, an immense comfort to know simply that Jesus Christ suffered and died for your sins. On Good Friday, you are assured that you deserve the place of Jesus. The penalty for your sin is death and eternal condemnation. That penalty has been removed. Jesus has taken your place. What a comfort to hear the words of Jesus: "It is finished" (John 19:30). So, at the end of the day on Good Friday, it might seem like you could have justifying faith in Jesus Christ as the one who fully paid for your sins. But ask yourself this: if you knew that the body of Jesus Christ had decayed in that tomb, and that was the end of his earthly story, would doubts not begin to eat away at your faith? Maybe his death in your place didn't work. Or maybe he's still working on your forgiveness. Your punishment is, after all, *eternal* condemnation. Perhaps your penalty will never truly be completely paid off.[6]

This is why you need to know about the resurrection of Jesus in order to be justified. By raising Jesus from the dead, God delivers you from those doubts that would destroy your faith and deprive you of the righteousness that comes through it. Jesus has risen! His resurrection is like a second "It is finished." It is a confirmation that your penalty for sin *is* completely paid off. Jesus died for you, and he is risen. At Easter, Jesus assures you that you are united to the one who has completed your forgiveness. Union with the risen Jesus Christ includes a firm, justifying faith in his completed work.

---

5. Gross, *Living the Christian Year*, 188–89.
6. Ursinus, *Commentary*, 237.

Worship, Mission, and the Church Year

Transformation for Service

God's deliverance in the exodus is also a deliverance for the Israelites so that they can serve and worship him. God transfers the Israelites from their service to the Egyptians to service to him. In the Hebrew text, there is a play on words around the term for "service." The Israelites are trapped in "servitude" (Exod 2:23), and God demands that they be released so they can "serve" him (Exod 4:22).[7] When Moses and Aaron told Pharaoh, "Let my people go," the stated purpose for letting the Israelites go was a kind of service—a worship service. Their God wanted them to worship him in the desert (Exod 5:1–5). This is why they insisted that they be able to bring their livestock: for the required sacrifices (Exod 10:21–29). God delivered the Israelites from their service to Pharaoh so that they could be completely devoted to serving and worshiping him.

The resurrection accomplishes something similar for those who are united to Jesus. The resurrection of Jesus is about our transformation—"the presence of Christ within us and the power of Christ to change us."[8] Because Jesus is risen, we rise to new life, serving God with our whole lives. We who are united to Jesus are united to him in his resurrection (Rom 6:5). This means that we are set free from our slavery to sin (Rom 6:6), have risen to a new slavery—service to God (Rom 6:18), and now devoted our whole lives to this service, this worship: "offer your bodies as living sacrifices, holy and pleasing to God—this is your true and proper worship" (Rom 12:1).

In union with the risen Christ, we are set free to serve God. On the one hand, this happens through a greater confidence in our faith. The resurrection becomes a testimony to us and the whole world that our Savior has the power to set us free from our slavery to sin. Anyone who has struggled with an addiction or a temptation they cannot seem to resist knows what it is like to doubt this. We are trapped. We have tried so hard to resist temptation when we face it. We have even taken steps to avoid facing that temptation in the first place. Even so, we have fallen into it again and again. "Who will rescue [us] from this body that is subject to death?" (Rom 7:24). Jesus Christ rose from death. He has the power to set us free, for "it was impossible for death to keep its hold on him" (Acts 2:24). The resurrection proves it to us and the world—Jesus Christ has the power to free us. And

---

7. Wright, *Mission of God*, 269–70.
8. Gross, *Living the Christian Year*, 189.

in union with him, we begin to believe it. This is what union with a risen Christ does to our faith.

We are also set free to worship God through union with a risen Christ because of what that resurrection does to our former oppressors. In the resurrection, Jesus delivers a verdict against our oppressors and strips them of their power. John Murray called this the "juridical aspect of deliverance from the power of sin":[9]

> [I]t is by virtue of our having died with Christ, and our being raised with him in his resurrection from the dead, that the decisive breach with sin in its power, control, and defilement has been wrought, and . . . the reason for this is that Christ in his death and resurrection broke the power of sin, triumphed over the god of this world, the prince of darkness, executed judgment upon the world and its ruler, and by that victory delivered all those who were united to him form the power of darkness, and translated them into his own kingdom.[10]

All this is ours—the defeat our of spiritual oppressors—because Jesus rose from the dead and because we are united to him.

Our union with Jesus Christ in his resurrection also does something to us. It empowers us spiritually for holy living in service to God. Paul writes: "And if the Spirit of him who raised Jesus from the dead is living in you, he who raised Christ from the dead will also give life to your mortal bodies because of his Spirit who lives in you" (Rom 8:11). This union that we have with him is a real, organic union. As though we are branches in a vine, Jesus tells us, "Remain in me, as I also remain in you. No branch can bear fruit by itself; it must remain in the vine. Neither can you bear fruit unless you remain in me" (John 15:4). It is through our living union with Jesus Christ that we bear the fruit of service and worship, and "living" is key here. We cannot have this organic sanctifying union with Christ if he is not alive. Our union with the risen Jesus Christ includes, then, this second dimension of deliverance—rising to a new life of service to and worship of God—in addition to the first dimension—righteousness by faith.

---

9. Murray, "Agency in Definitive Sanctification," 288.
10. Ibid.

Worship, Mission, and the Church Year

The Resurrection of the Body

Union with the risen Jesus Christ involves a third dimension of deliverance. This might be the most obvious dimension of deliverance in the story of the exodus: the Israelites were delivered from the physical realities of their oppression. These physical realities involved their lives, their freedom, and their livelihoods.[11] The lives of the Israelites were threatened. The pharaoh had instructed the midwives to kill all the baby boys at the beginning of Moses' life. This threat to their lives continued (Exod 5:21), but at the Passover, God rescued them from this threat. After all, when the plague hit every firstborn in Egypt, the Israelites were spared (Exod 12:12–13). The Israelites were oppressed politically, as foreigners in Egypt without a voice, without power, and without freedom. God delivered them from the hand of Pharaoh—a man who represents political oppressors in every age. At the time of the Passover, Pharaoh begged them to leave (Exod 12:31–32)! They were oppressed economically; they were forced into slavery and denied their livelihoods. As the situation worsened, they were forced to do more work and told they were lazy when they couldn't keep up the pace. God delivered them from this economic injustice—the sort of economic injustice we see all the time. At the time of the Passover, the Egyptians even gave them silver, gold, and clothing. It almost seems like back-pay (Exod 12:36). When God delivers his people, he delivers them physically—life, freedom, and livelihood.

The resurrection is also about physical deliverance. It is about the "hope for the resurrection of the body."[12] Two phrases in the Apostles' Creed are not often enough clearly distinguished—"the resurrection of the body" and "the life everlasting." When a whole congregation sings on Easter Charles Wesley's "Christ the Lord Is Risen Today," they belt out the line: "Christ has opened paradise. Alleluia!" What proportion of them is thinking about eternal life, and what proportion is thinking about the resurrection of the body? Too many worshipers would probably respond to this question by asking, "What do you mean? There's a difference?" In the popular imagination, how much a difference is there between the bodily resurrection and eternal life? Unfortunately, when these two realities are collapsed together, it is the bodily resurrection that tends to be ignored. Easter is a good time to focus especially on it. (In this book, eternal life in the kingdom of God will

---

11. Wright, *Mission of God*, 268–72.
12. Gross, *Living the Christian Year*, 189.

be considered later, as an Advent theme.) The resurrection of Jesus Christ is about God delivering our created bodies.

This hope for our physical bodies is a smaller part of the hope that God has given the whole created world. God communicated his compassion for creation at the time of the flood. With the sign of the rainbow, God made a covenant never to destroy the earth again with a flood. This was a covenant not just with Noah and his family but "with every living creature that was with you—the birds, the livestock, and all the wild animals, all those that came out of the ark with you—every living creature on earth" (Gen 9:10). God has promised all creation that he is committed to it—preserving it and restoring it.[13] That is the world's hope. The Bible paints a picture of God's future for creation. God will make creation a place of peace and flourishing life (Isa 65). God will purge creation of all sin and evil (2 Pet 3). His purpose for doing all of this is the praise of his name. When God promises to give us glorified bodies, he is promising to put us into proper communion with creation so that we glorify God together.[14]

This happens through union with the risen Jesus Christ. This is the great theme of 1 Corinthians 15—to be united to Jesus Christ in his resurrection is to be promised a glorified body like his. Jesus is risen. That doesn't only mean that he has accomplished the sacrifice for your sins to make you righteous before God. That doesn't only mean that he has risen so that you can be set free from your bondage to sin. The resurrection of Jesus Christ is about hope for your own physical body. When people are altogether too focused on themselves, we accuse them of "navel-gazing." Navel-gazing is a bad thing. But the resurrection of Jesus Christ actually encourages us to navel-gaze in a certain way. As people united to a risen Christ, we can look at our navels (and the rest of our bodies) in a new light. Our bodies will be changed. We will have glorified bodies that fit right in with a restored creation. These bodies will be like his. Jesus Christ is the "firstborn over all creation" and the "firstborn from among the dead," and through him God would "reconcile to himself all things, whether things on earth or things in heaven, by making peace through his blood, shed on the cross" (Col 1:15–20). Being united to a risen Jesus Christ means having the hope that these broken bodies will not be our last bodies. In union with a risen Christ, we live in the hope of the resurrection of the body.

---

13. Wright, *Mission of God*, 326.
14. Wright, *Mission of God*, 404–12; Wright, *Mission of God's People*, 53–55.

Mission in Union with the Risen Christ

Our union with the risen Jesus Christ includes all three of these dimensions:

- Righteousness by faith
- Rising to a new life of service to and worship of God, and
- Resurrection of the body to glorify God with all creation.

What does all of this have to do with our missional work—our work as Christians among our neighbors in the world? How is mission possible only because we are united to a risen Jesus Christ? Our mission is about all the dimensions of deliverance because we are united to a Savior whose mission in his resurrection is multi-dimensional: "our commitment to mission must demonstrate the same broad totality of concern for human need that God demonstrated in what he did for Israel."[15] Let's take in order the three dimensions of union with our risen Christ we identified above.

The Mission of Righteousness by Faith

Mission happens in union with Jesus Christ, risen in vicarious righteousness. Because he rose from the dead, and because we are united to him by faith, his righteousness is credited to us. Personally, this means that we do not live in guilt and shame but in confidence before God. Missionally—as we head out into the world—it means that we aren't braggarts. We're righteous before God "not by works, so that no one can boast" (Eph 2:9). We're not even the kind of silent braggarts who salivate at the thought of other people noticing what great Christians we are. A person who is sent out into the world in union with the risen Jesus Christ doesn't need to brag or have their righteousness noticed by others, because the resurrection of Jesus confirms that Jesus is their righteousness. After all, if a person believes that Jesus Christ rose from the dead and has completed their forgiveness and the imputation of righteousness to them, then why would they feel the need for the world to notice and affirm their righteousness? Didn't Jesus rise from the dead? Isn't that affirmation enough? Union with a risen Jesus Christ means that we go out into the world happy to do our acts of righteousness in secret, as Jesus instructed (Matt 6:1). Missional union with the risen Christ is about humility.

---

15. Wright, *Mission of God*, 275.

This dimension of union with the risen Christ doesn't just impact how we view ourselves out in the world—whether we think we deserve praise for our righteousness. Union with the risen Christ also impacts how we view other people in the world. We approach them differently. We treat them differently than we would have if Christ had not risen and confirmed that true righteousness before God is only found in him. The current toxic and highly polarized political environment in the United States provides American Christians with daily opportunities to practice this. Our culture insists that the person with a different political viewpoint is ill-informed, foolish, and even revolting. Agreeing with my political opinion is righteousness. And if someone disagrees with my righteous position, I should treat them as their unrighteousness deserves. That attitude withers in union with the risen Jesus Christ. Christian mission begins to focus on reconciliation because the resurrection is about peace and perfection. Frost uses the concept of peace in describing a passion for restoring relationships as a component of a missional mindset: "Because we have peace with God, we are commissioned to demonstrate it to others by making peace with each other and the world."[16] Jesus Christ perfected our peace with God in his resurrection. In the resurrection, Jesus confirms that he is the *only* source of righteousness before God. Only through union with him are sins forgiven and perfect righteousness before God granted. The person united to Christ simply cannot view others as righteous and unrighteous, good and evil. "Viewed in themselves, one's neighbors may not appear worthy of love. But just as Christians are called to live not in themselves but in Christ, the law of God calls Christians to consider their neighbors not 'in themselves' but in relation to God."[17] In union with a risen Christ, we see everyone—even with radically different political positions—as more similar to us than dissimilar. The mission of union with Christ in light of his perfect righteousness is a mission of humility and reconciliation.

The Mission of Rising to New Life

The second dimension of union with the risen Christ is the new life which glorifies God. This new life relates to our mission as Christians in two ways: living a God-glorifying life makes a difference in the world, and living a God-glorifying life is attractive to people in our world. Recall the

16. Frost, *The Road to Missional*, 104.
17. Billings, *Union with Christ*, 111.

connection between the exodus and the resurrection—both are major acts of deliverance by God, and they share many of the same themes. In both the exodus and the resurrection, God's redeemed people make a difference in the world because they begin to imitate God's desire for redemption. The Israelites were redeemed in the exodus, and this made them both redeemed and redeeming people.[18] The Israelites became released slaves, and God's subsequent laws instructed them to treat their own slaves accordingly: "[I]n the seventh year you must let them go free. . . . Remember that you were slaves in Egypt and the LORD your God redeemed you. That is why I give you this command today" (Deut 15:12, 15). The Israelites were rescued from oppression and poverty, and God then made them people who cared for the oppressed. After an instruction to treat immigrants, orphans, and widows well, we read: "Remember that you were slaves in Egypt and the LORD your God redeemed you from there. That is why I command you to do this" (Deut 24:18). In Leviticus 25, God gives instructions for the Year of Jubilee, a practice that would protect Israel from generational poverty and wealth inequality,[19] and God repeatedly associates this practice with Israel's identity as a people redeemed from slavery in Egypt (verses 38, 42, 55). Their identity as redeemed people extends even to the way they treat foreigners: "Do not oppress a foreigner; you yourselves know how it feels to be foreigners, because you were foreigners in Egypt" (Exod 23:9).

The mission of those redeemed in the exodus is similar to the mission of those redeemed in the resurrection. When we are sent out into the world in new life through union with a risen Jesus Christ, we are sent out to change the world. Several of the same themes arise—the reality of being redeemed in Jesus Christ is reflected in the Christian's treatment of slaves (Eph 6:9), the poor and oppressed (1 John 3:16–17), those who are indebted, financially or otherwise (Matt 18:21–35; Luke 6:36; Eph 4:32; Col 3:13), and foreigners (Acts 10). People in union with a risen Jesus Christ practice the realities of the resurrection in the way they treat others in new life.

Living a God-glorifying life in union with the risen Jesus Christ also attracts the world. God raises us to new life so that we attract the world's curiosity, the world's hopes, the world's admiration, and the world's worship, and the world's approval.[20] All of this attraction is not so much attraction to us, but to God. Many of us have witnessed the world's attention being

---

18. Wright, *Mission of God's People*, 106–8.
19. Wright, *Mission of God*, 290–96.
20. Wright, *Mission of God's People*, 128–47.

drawn to a Christian community after their surprisingly gracious response to a tragedy. A shooter murders Amish children, and the Christian community forgives.[21] Terrorists kill Christians in majority-Muslim countries, and the Christian community forgives.[22] These counterintuitive acts of forgiveness are part of the new life that Christians live in union with the risen Jesus Christ, and this new life is attractive. I remember witnessing this one-on-one as I helped a man profess faith in Jesus Christ. He said that the hope and confidence of his Christian parents and grandparents attracted him. His family members had lived that new life in union with a risen Jesus Christ, and their example became a part of the church's mission. The mission of union with a risen Jesus Christ is a mission in which our rising to new, God-glorifying life changes and attracts the world.

The Mission of the Resurrection of the Body

The third dimension of union with the risen Jesus Christ is the hope of the resurrection of the body. The resurrection of the body is about the hope of all creation. This is a focus for God's mission and for the church's mission. When Wright describes how to read the Bible missionally, he includes this: we should read every text "in the light of God's purpose for his whole creation, including the redemption of humanity and the creation of the new heavens and new earth."[23] Likewise, the missional church movement has often embraced this as its central question: "What is God doing *in the world*?"[24] To be missional is to ask not just about what God is doing in human hearts. To be missional is to be concerned with the hope for the created world, and nothing focuses us on this hope more than our hope of the resurrection of the body in union with the risen Jesus Christ.

God's people have had this hope as a central part of their mission for millennia. When God warned his people in the Old Testament not to worship created things like so many of the nations around them, it wasn't because God thought his people should be concerned with spiritual things and not earthly things. Rather, God wanted his people to recognize the distinction between Creator and creation so that they could appropriately

---

21. Kraybill et al., "Amish Grace."
22. Casper, "Forgiveness."
23. Wright, *Mission of God*, 67.
24. VanGelder and Zscheile, *Missional Church in Perspective*, 113. Emphasis added.

value the creation as something holy.[25] This respect for God's creation is part of humanity's original task. God put Adam in the Garden of Eden, in the created world, "to serve and protect" (Gen 2:15). Wright calls this the "ecological dimension of mission,"[26] and he uses the metaphor of a tenant hiring renovations done in a rented property. Suppose the contractor hesitates before doing the work, "Is the landlord okay with this?" The tenant can point to the landlord's written authorization proving that the tenant is getting the work done on the landlord's behalf.[27] A pastor living in a church-owned parsonage might be an even better metaphor. As I get authorization to renovate a bathroom, I'm doing so not just as an agent of the landlord, the church. I'm doing this as a member of the body that benefits from this renovated bathroom. The rest of the church wants me to have a comfortable home. And even if I'm personally indifferent to the renovations, at some point in the future some other pastor will probably be living in this same house, and I want that pastor to feel at home. In a very tiny way, the renovation of this bathroom is part of the whole community's mission, and mine too. It's not just about me carrying out the landlord's wishes. It's about who I am as a member of a community with hopes for the future.

In a similar way, Christians who are united to the risen Christ and have the hope of the resurrection of the body engage in this ecological dimension of mission with a view toward that restored creation they are part of. There's a temptation to engage in the care of creation in nostalgia and fear. Every week brings a new story about climate change, threatened and extinct species, or the pollution of rivers and lakes. Our world tells us to fight to recover the past. Our world tells us to fear the death of our world and our own bodies. As Christians we should be working alongside our neighbors when they are concerned for creation, but we should do so in hope and yearning.[28] We are united to the risen Jesus Christ. He has overcome death. He has risen. We are united to him and have the promise of our own resurrection. Our bodies will be part of that glorified creation we long for. We put on our gardening gloves looking forward.

As we are sent out into the created world, our mission is directed especially at other human beings. Our hope of the resurrection of the body impacts how we treat other people in our created world. We haven't been

---

25. Wright, *Mission of God*, 400–403.
26. Ibid., 327.
27. Ibid., 404.
28. Ibid., 409.

sent out into our neighborhoods and forests to rescue only the souls of our neighbors. Our mission isn't to bring people out of the world. Our mission occurs within the created world.[29] Because we are united to the risen Jesus Christ (risen in a physical body), our hope for other people is about their bodies as much as it is about their souls. This has implications for the work of our bodies. As Christians, our mission is aimed at art[30]—because art is part of creation and proceeds from human bodies. As Christians, our mission is aimed at the culture[31]—for culture also is part of creation and proceeds from human bodies. We are united to Jesus Christ. He took upon himself the creational body of a human person in Jesus Christ. And he rose from the dead to perfect that creational body. That perfection involves a glorified human body, the shimmering beauty of perfect art (Rev 1:13–16), and the community of a perfect culture (Rev 4). The church is sent out in mission united to a risen Christ who promises us our own resurrection of the body and the restoration of the whole creation. Missional union with Christ means having a passion for the good of the created world—life, art, and culture—and yearning for that perfection that the resurrection promises.

In these ways, the church's mission is shaped by our union with a risen Jesus Christ. His resurrection propels us to see reconciliation with others because we know our righteousness is only in the risen Christ. His resurrection empowers us to live a new life which changes the world and attracts the attention of the world. His resurrection gives us a hope for our own bodies and for creation itself, as we engage with our neighbors who are concerned for the good of life, art, and culture.

Missional Liturgy for Easter

Easter Liturgies can be part of our formation for mission in union with our risen Christ. Below are some ideas. They are grouped according to the three dimensions of mission in union with the risen Christ identified above.

---

29. VanGelder and Zscheile, *Missional Church in Perspective*, 113–14.
30. Frost, *Road to Missional*, 111–12.
31. VanGelder and Zscheile, *Missional Church in Perspective*, 136.

Worship, Mission, and the Church Year

Righteousness

At Easter, worshipers gather for union with Jesus Christ. He is risen, and through his resurrection he has completed the forgiveness of sins. Worshipers will be sent out to engage in mission as people who humbly recognize that everyone they meet has the same need they do: to find righteousness not in themselves, but in Jesus Christ. Here are some ways the liturgy can shape worshipers for mission according to this aspect of union with Christ:

1. Prayer

Prayers during Easter can help worshipers practice humbly seeing others in the world as potential recipients of the perfect righteousness and completed forgiveness of the risen Jesus Christ. This can be explicitly stated in the text of the prayers:

- "You have completed our forgiveness. Help us to see that we and our neighbors together need the forgiveness that you have completed."
- "Send us out from here confident before the world, not because we are righteous, but because you, our risen Jesus Christ, are perfectly righteous for us."

This can also be accomplished by praying for those whom the congregation might otherwise scorn. Imagine a congregation that has resisted the legalization of same-sex marriage. What happens when this congregation offers a prayer for the LGBT community? Imagine a congregation that has often mobilized for gun control in their murder-racked city. What happens when they pray together for the safety of gun-rights advocates who are demonstrating that weekend? When a congregation offers sincere prayers for the people who are their enemies, culturally speaking, they practice seeing others not as threats but as potential recipients of the righteousness of the risen Christ. They practice mission in union with the risen Christ.

In fact, God has instructed the church to offer precisely these kinds of prayers—missional prayers for outsiders on account of the unique and perfect righteousness of the risen Christ:

> I urge, then, first of all, that petitions, prayers, intercession and thanksgiving be made for all people—for kings and all those in authority, that we may live peaceful and quiet lives in all godliness and holiness. This is good, and pleases God our Savior, who wants

all people to be saved and to come to a knowledge of the truth. For there is one God and one mediator between God and mankind, the man Christ Jesus, who gave himself as a ransom for all people. (1 Tim 2:1–6)

The Canons of the Synod of Dort, used by Dutch Reformed churches, encourages the church to pray humbly for those who have not yet received the perfect righteousness of the risen Jesus Christ: "for others who have not yet been called, we are to pray to the God who calls things that do not exist as though they did. In no way, however, are we to pride ourselves as better than they, as though we had distinguished ourselves from them."[32] The celebration of the resurrection empowers this kind of prayer, teaching us to see our salvation not as something we have accomplished, distinguishing ourselves from the world, but something that Jesus Christ has accomplished for us.

2. Liturgies of Reconciliation

Worship can form a congregation for mission in union with a risen Christ when liturgies of reconciliation are included.[33] Some liturgies lead congregations to practice reconciliation with one another on account of the completed forgiveness of Jesus Christ. Words to this effect can be included in the invitation to eat and drink from the table or in a prayer of thanks for the work of Jesus Christ: because Jesus Christ has completed the reconciliation between sinners and God through his body and blood, we who eat from this table are reconciled with one another.[34] In fact, attempting to celebrate the Lord's Supper while divisions remain within the body of Christ is a contradiction, which Paul himself writes on account of the divisions in Corinth: "when you come together, it is not the Lord's Supper you eat" (1 Cor 11:20). Likewise, when the Lord's Super is truly celebrated, it is a meal of unity created by union with Jesus Christ.[35] Perhaps the words don't even have to be spoken. Worshipers learn what it means to have missional union with the risen Christ as they eat and drink from the same table together, especially through practices that emphasize the communal aspect

---

32. "Canons of Dort," III/IV, Article 15.
33. Meyers, "Liturgy," 49.
34. For example, *Service for the Lord's Day*, 96.
35. Billings, *Union with Christ*, 100–103.

of communion (rather than individualizing practices like dipping the bread into the wine one-by-one).

The liturgy of confession and forgiveness can form worshipers for missional union with the risen Christ. When worshipers receive forgiveness in worship through union with Jesus who completed forgiveness in his resurrection, these worshipers are empowered to go out into the world on a mission of forgiveness. "Because we know God's forgiveness, we are able to offer forgiveness to others."[36]

This can happen through other acts of reconciliation. One example is the "passing of the peace," when each worshiper is charged to clasp the hands of worshipers nearby and speak a word of peace to them: "the peace of Christ be with you." Meyers connects this to missional union with Christ: "in a missional congregation its exchange in the assembly will reflect the congregation's concern for peacemaking in the world and its participation in God's mission of reconciliation."[37] Some churches will have a time of "mutual greeting," which is similar. Worshipers say "hello" to one another. This might seem to accomplish the same thing—helping worshipers practice missional union with Jesus. On the other hand, a "mutual greeting" can easily become nothing more than a mutual greeting—a polite "hello" to neighbors—rather than an meaningful participation in the unity created by the completed sacrifice of Christ. The same thing can happen with "passing the peace." Eventually, saying "peace" to the people around you is nothing more than a churchy way of saying a polite "hello." The liturgy can teach worshipers the habit of being sent out in union with Jesus who has risen in perfected reconciliation, but not if the theological core of the ritual action is replaced with a cultural convention.

Prayers and liturgies of reconciliation like the Lord's Supper, the confession and forgiveness, and the passing of the peace are ways that worshipers are formed for union with a risen Christ as they are sent out into the world. These liturgical elements place worshipers in the humble position of receiving complete forgiveness and perfect righteousness before God only through the reconciling work of Jesus Christ completed in the resurrection. Worshipers who learn that humility are then sent out into the world to see others as all potential recipients of this same forgiving and reconciling grace of the risen Jesus Christ.

---

36. Meyers, *Missional Worship*, 143.
37. Ibid., 146.

The Resurrection of Jesus
New Life

Jesus Christ is risen. We know that God is more powerful than the worst powers of death that enslave us; in fact, the powers that enslave us have been disarmed, and we are empowered for a new kind of living through a spiritual union with a living Savior. Jesus Christ is risen, and we who are united to him have a new life—one which changes the world and attracts the world. As we gather for worship, we are shaped for mission according to this new life.

Missional union with a risen Christ involves a new life that changes the world. Liturgy can shape worshipers for this. Mark Labberton describes multiple facets of world-changing worship.[38] In worship, we acknowledge that Jesus is Lord in a world where so many other powers demand to be worshiped. In worship, the church experiences what it means to be in the world and not of the world. In worship, we catch a glimpse of the very real changed world that the resurrection accomplishes. Liturgy that is bold in all of these ways is liturgy that equips worshipers to live a world-changing new life in the risen Christ. Every so often, I find myself shaking as I begin worship on a Sunday morning because I have planned to step out on a limb. I'm going to issue an unusually direct challenge or chastisement to the worshipers. I'm going to speak more plainly than usual about some happening in the world. I'm going to declare that something is sin or evil. And I'm honestly not quite sure how the worshipers will take it. I'm going to challenge the powers. Perhaps these are some of the moments that form worshipers to live a world-changing new life in the risen Christ. I know these moments form me.

As the church worships, it also lives a new life in Christ that is attractive. Christopher Wright says, "The praise of God's people is missional."[39] This has been true since the beginning. Psalm 96 is one psalm that makes this attractive purpose of worship clear.

> Sing to the LORD a new song;
>   sing to the LORD, all the earth.
> Sing to the LORD, praise his name;
>   proclaim his salvation day after day.
> Declare his glory among the nations,
>   his marvelous deeds among all peoples.

---

38. Labberton, *Dangerous Act.*
39. Wright, *Mission of God's People*, 250.

> For great is the LORD and most worthy of praise;
>   he is to be feared above all gods.
> For all the gods of the nations are idols,
>   but the LORD made the heavens.
> Splendor and majesty are before him;
>   strength and glory are in his sanctuary.
> Ascribe to the LORD, all you families of nations,
>   ascribe to the LORD glory and strength.
> Ascribe to the LORD the glory due his name;
>   bring an offering and come into his courts.
> Worship the LORD in the splendor of his holiness;
>   tremble before him, all the earth. (Ps 96:1–9)

The worship of God's people in the Old Testament had the goal of attracting the nations to worship God. The primary purpose of worship is ascribing glory to God, but a secondary purpose is to draw others to worship God.[40] Linford L. Stutzman and George R. Hunsberger describe the attractiveness worship of missional congregations they visited for one study. It wasn't so much that elements or circumstances of worship, like the musical style, were engineered to physically attract outsiders as additional bodies in the pews. If worship in these missional churches was attractive, it was because it was directed to God and was a public witness to his grace and what it means in our world.[41] If a congregation worships a certain way, and attendance consequentially grows, the worship is attractive. However, worship that displays the attractiveness of new life through union with the risen Christ is attractive even if attendance is stagnant or declines. It's attractive not because it accomplishes attraction, but because it shows God's deliverance to a world that needs it.

Worshipers can learn to live in the public attractiveness of this new life in direct ways. Worship leaders can use language, symbols, and signs accessible to the neighbors in the local context. This is missional inasmuch as it allows worship to be more public. The worship itself can be more easily understood by the surrounding world.[42] When worship leaders connect mission and worship in a direct way like this, worshipers begin to live into the connection between their own new life in Christ and the attractiveness

---

40. Wright, *Mission of God's People*, 250–51.
41. Stutzman and Hunsberger, "Public Witness," 100–116.
42. Townley, *Missional Worship*, 107–15.

of this life to the world.⁴³ Worshipers can learn to live and speak in ways that more clearly display what new life in Christ looks like to their own neighbors. However, learning to live into the attractiveness of new life in Christ in worship is something that happens more in subtle ways. Worshipers learn to be people who, as those risen to new life in the risen Christ, display "love, joy, peace, patience, kindness, goodness, faithfulness, gentleness, and self-control" (Gal 5:22–23). Through the liturgy, worshipers participate in new life in union with a risen Christ which changes the world and is attractive.

Resurrection of the Body

Jesus rose from the dead with a body that belongs to the perfected created world. As the church is sent out into the world, we are united to this glorified, bodily Christ, and thereby we have a passion for the created world to be set right. This includes everything—our bodies, human culture and art, and the natural world. Easter liturgy can help shape us for this focus on the perfected creation.

Prayer is, once again, a natural liturgical place for this. At Easter, worshipers can be led in prayer for the restoration of creation, acknowledging that the resurrection is about created things. The décor and circumstances of worship can also orient worshipers toward hope for the created world. While giving advice to individuals for their own celebration of the resurrection, Gross suggests getting outside, taking a walk through a park.⁴⁴ How can the created world become more noticeable in worship at Easter? Decorating with flowers and living plants in worship is appropriate.⁴⁵ A congregation's climate will determine other possibilities—worshiping outdoors may be a possibility. It is important to pair these signs of natural life with words that connect the resurrection to the hope for creation—especially in the Northern Hemisphere where directing the congregation's attention to the created world at Easter threatens to turn the season into a celebration of springtime, rather than the eternal renewal of the resurrection of the body and the new creation. For this reason, it might be good for the circumstances of worship to remind worshipers not only of the life present in the current creation, but also of the current creation's need for life.

---

43. Schmit, *Sent and Gathered*, 125.
44. Gross, *Living the Christian Year*, 196.
45. Ibid., 195.

Liturgy at Easter can also focus on human bodies, culture, and art. In a certain way, the entire Christian life is an art project. "We are all striving together to become works of art that are pleasing to God and examples to the world."[46] The use of the arts in worship is especially important, not so much because art has value in itself, though it does, but because art can direct our attention to God's grace.[47] It does this in part by giving worshipers a glimpse of the renewal of our humanity in the resurrection of Jesus Christ. The arts in worship are enacted metaphors for our own bodies in service to God throughout the week. This is why the music used in worship should especially support the instrument of the human voice.[48] Even the elements of the Lord's Supper can help to orient us toward this mission in the resurrection of Jesus. The Lord's Supper uses the products of human artistry and industry—farming, baking, wine-making—for a holy purpose.[49] That itself points to the hope of the resurrection of the body. To use the artistry of sound, movement, and sight to direct our attention to the glory of God is to incorporate us liturgically into God's mission in Jesus Christ—a mission which ends with all creation, restored through Christ's resurrection, glorifying God.

---

46. Benson, *Liturgy*, 134.

47. Ibid., 134.

48. Schmit, *Sent and Gathered*, 164–65.

49. Meyers, *Missional Worship*, 164–65, 175; Smith, *Desiring the Kingdom*, 199–200; Davies, *Worship and Mission*, 100.

five

The Ascension of Jesus

Are you confident that your place in the world and your hard work is meaningful in the mission of God? Some of the members of my church seemed to be searching for that confidence when we participated in some question-and-answer sessions with a representative from a local charity that serves families who are homeless. We were exploring what it would mean for us to get involved, and the question on the minds of some of the members of my community seemed to be this: "Would our hard work have a meaningful place in the mission of God if we volunteered for this organization?" This led to an awkward exchange. The awkwardness arose because this non-profit works with churches, but it is not a specifically Christian organization. When Christians volunteer for an organization that has an explicitly Christian mission—one that looks to the verbal proclamation of the gospel and discipling people toward saving faith—missional confidence comes much easier. But that wasn't the case with this organization. A deacon asked, "How many people have come to faith in Jesus through this program?" Well, none, directly. That's not the focus of the program. "Are you telling us we can't share our faith with the people we serve?" Not exactly, but the charity's purpose isn't to encourage or equip us for this. The organization is focused on meeting immediate earthly needs in love. These are important questions, because their answers have something to do with how our work relates to the broader mission of God in Jesus Christ.

This challenge—figuring out how ordinary work fits into the mission of God—is something many of us struggle with. Maybe the majority of the good work you do is done in cooperation with neighbors and organizations that don't share your Christian mission. Are you really sure that your hard work can contribute to God's mission in Jesus Christ? Are you confident?

This chapter is about that confidence and the opposing anxiety. The chapter won't focus on strategies for doing good work in a secular world but on the confidence we should have that our good work is part of God's mission. For that confidence, we need to have union with Jesus Christ. Specifically, we need to have union with an ascended Jesus Christ. Because Jesus Christ is in heaven, and we are united to him, we can be confident that our prayers go up and that the power of God comes down. When we worship in union with a Christ who pleads for us and pours out his Holy Spirit, we practice being part of something bigger, something that includes an almighty God, in fact, that is driven by an almighty God. Worship that focuses on the ascension and Pentecost offers liturgical opportunities for the church to learn the habit of missional confidence.

United to the Ascended Christ

"[H]e was taken up before their very eyes, and a cloud hid him from their sight" (Acts 1:9). The story of the ascension has strange dimensions—quite literally. Jesus, in his physical body, rose from the ground and went, we're told, to heaven. In the last century, we have been there—above the clouds—and we haven't seen heaven, much less Jesus in his physical body. And it isn't just that astronauts have served as representatives of humanity, going up there and reporting back. Many of us have personally ascended above the clouds squeezed next to strangers on tiny seats in airplanes. If we've had the luxury of the window seat, we've personally seen "the heavens." But we haven't found the "heaven" where Jesus is in his body. The physical reality of the story is hard to understand. It's a mystery of the Christian faith whose details are beyond the orbit of this book.[1]

Within the orbit of this book, however, is this striking claim: "God raised us up with Christ and seated us with him in the heavenly realms in Christ Jesus . . ." (Eph 2:6). Whatever could that mean? God was doing this with us long before we boarded airplanes and space shuttles. In what ways are we ascended with Christ and seated with Christ? Jesus also makes a striking claim going the other direction—that he would be down here on earth, with us even after his ascension: "I am with you always, to the very end of the age" (Matt 28:20); "I will not leave you as orphans; I will come to you" (John 14:18).

---

1. Readers interested in exploring that question a little further should read Parry, *The Biblical Cosmos*, 184–88.

The Ascension of Jesus

What can these things mean? In what way are we seated with Christ in heaven, and in what way is he with us here on earth? For the answer, look at the consequences: what happens to us because we are "raised with Christ" and because he is "with us always"? There are three main consequences of being united to an ascended Jesus Christ. First, his ascension assures us of his return. He promised that he was going to his Father's house "to prepare a place" for us. "And if I go and prepare a place for you, I will come back and take you to be with me that you also may be where I am" (John 14:2–3). Second, if we are united to him and he is in heaven, this means that he is there to intercede for us: "Christ Jesus who died—more than that, who was raised to life—is at the right hand of God and is also interceding for us" (Rom 8:34). Third, because Jesus Christ ascended to heaven and we are united to him, we have assurance that he pours out his gifts on us: "But to each one of us grace has been given as Christ apportioned it. This is why it says: 'When he ascended on high, he took many captives and gave gifts to his people'" (Eph 4:7–8).

That first consequence—we have confidence that Jesus will take us where he is—that's important. There are compelling reasons to keep the ascension closely linked with the return of Christ. Jesus himself linked these two things.[2] The next chapter will be entirely devoted to the promised return of Jesus. For now, let's focus on the second and third consequences of union with an ascended Jesus. Jesus is in heaven and we belong to him by faith. Because of this, we can have confidence first that he is interceding for us and second that he has sent his Holy Spirit to give us gifts. In other words, we can be confident that our prayers go up and that the power of God comes down.

Our Prayers Go Up

"Christ's ascension means that in heaven there is one who, knowing first-hand the experience of suffering and temptation, prays for us and perfects our prayers."[3] Jesus intercedes when we confess our sins and plead for forgiveness. The book of Hebrews tells us again and again what it means that Jesus is our intercessor: he provided the sacrifice for our sins and then ascended to heaven. He is doing the work of the Great High Priest: he made the perfect sacrifice, and now he is appearing before God to have the merits

---

2. See John 14 and Farrow, *Ascension and Ecclesia*, 265.
3. *Worship Sourcebook*, 661.

of that sacrifice applied to us (Heb 4:14; 6:19; 8:4; 9:14). The work of this priest, like every priest, is especially about our purification before God, our cleansing, the forgiveness of our sins. This is the gospel of the ascension: "God exalted him to his own right hand as Prince and Savior that he might give repentance and forgiveness of sins to Israel" (Acts 5:31). Union with an ascended Jesus gives us confidence when we pray our prayers of confession.

How many of us prayed our first prayers of confession wondering whether God heard them and whether we were really forgiven? I remember overhearing a young child ask her parents a question like this: "I prayed that God would forgive me. How do I know he did?" I don't remember what the answer was, but it could have been this: "You can know that he forgives you because Jesus is in heaven." Through the perfect priestly intercession of Jesus Christ, our prayers are heard by God the Father and answered with his generous forgiveness—forgiveness for all sins, past, present, and future. That's what happens when we have union with an ascended Jesus Christ.

Don't imagine, however, that Jesus brings only prayers of confession to the Father's ear! Jesus wraps all of our prayers in his righteousness. He wants us to pray all our prayers with the same confidence. He made this point in the Parable of the Friend at Midnight (Luke 11:5–8): God is better than an annoyed neighbor. If even that annoyed neighbor will listen, surely God will! He made this point with the Parable of the Widow and the Unjust Judge (Luke 18:1–8): God is better than an unjust judge. If even that judge will answer a persistent widow, surely God will answer your prayers! In a number of places in the Gospels, Jesus is even quoted as saying something like: "You will receive whatever you ask for in prayer" (Matt 17:20; 21:22; Mark 9:29; 11:24; Luke 17:6; John 14:13; 15:7; 16:23).

That instruction—"ask whatever you wish in my name"—creates a thousand follow-up questions. Theologian David Crump convincingly argues that Jesus never teaches what is commonly assumed: that the "success" of our prayers will vary with the strength of our faith. Instead, Crump says, Jesus says this so that we will pray in Jesus' name, with the belief that God *can* grant us whatever we ask for, and with the trust that *in the end* the Father will give us everything good.[4]

When we twist the instructions that Jesus gave, our attention is focused on the strength of our faith and the objects of our requests to God. We look back and forth between the success of our prayers (Have I received what I asked for yet?) and the strength of our faith (Maybe I didn't believe

---

4. Crump, *Knocking on Heaven's Door*, 21–39, 158–78.

hard enough when I prayed). The result is always the same and the opposite of what Jesus intended: we end up being *less* confident in prayer. Instead, when we receive the instructions the way Jesus intended, we look at him when we pray. We trust that he is interceding for us and is in fact one with the God who is able and willing to give us what is good. The result is completely different: we have confidence in prayer. The ascension enables us to pray all of our petitions with confidence.

Jesus Christ is ascended, interceding for us at the right hand of God the Father. We should be looking toward Jesus when we pray, and that kind of prayer is confident prayer. If you are preoccupied with the strength of your faith, you're only going to wonder whether it could be stronger. If you are preoccupied with the objects of your requests, you're only going to be constantly evaluating whether you're really going to receive them. But union with Jesus Christ makes you into a person who prays differently. Through union with the ascended Jesus Christ, our petitions are lifted upward to heaven and we pray with confidence. That is the upward consequence of the ascension.

The Power of God Comes Down

The downward consequence of the ascension is the outpouring of the Holy Spirit. Jesus said, "Unless I go away, the Advocate will not come to you; but if I go, I will send him to you" (John 16:7). He repeated this promise at his ascension: "you will receive power when the Holy Spirit comes on you; and you will be my witnesses in Jerusalem, and in all Judea and Samaria, and to the ends of the earth" (Acts 1:8). Those promises were fulfilled at the festival of Pentecost. We shouldn't think of Pentecost as the beginning of the church. The church, as the elect people of God, has existed since creation. We shouldn't think of Pentecost as the beginning of the Holy Spirit's work. The Bible tells us about the Spirit of God working even since creation. Instead, we should think about Pentecost as the fulfillment of that promise of Jesus—the promise that after he left, he would equip the church with the power of God and his continuing presence. Pentecost is a consequence of Ascension Day. The ascension has even been called the "prelude to Pentecost."[5] We who are united to an ascended Jesus Christ receive the Holy Spirit.

---

5. *Worship Sourcebook*, 661.

This is a pattern that we see throughout the Bible: when the leader of the people of God departs, the successor receives a blessing and a commissioning to continue the work. At the time of Moses' death, Joshua was equipped to continue the work (Deut 31). At the time of Elijah's departure, Elisha was equipped with his mantle (2 Kgs 2). At the time of David's death, Solomon was equipped to continue on with the temple plans and begin the work of building (2 Chr 28–29). Now, the whole church is equipped with the Spirit of Jesus upon his ascension into heaven.

There is, of course, a major difference between Pentecost and the earlier stories. Amid the many similarities between the story of Elijah being taken up into heaven and the story of the ascension of Jesus in Luke 24, notice how the stories end. Here is 2 Kings 2:15: "The company of the prophets from Jericho, who were watching, said, 'The spirit of Elijah is resting on Elisha.' And they went to meet him and bowed to the ground before him." Those who were present offered their service to the successor. Now compare that carefully to Luke 24:52–53: "Then they worshiped him and returned to Jerusalem with great joy. And they stayed continually at the temple, praising God." Those who were present offered their worship to the one who ascended. The stories end differently because Jesus Christ is different than Elijah.

When Jesus Christ ascended to heaven and sent his Holy Spirit, the church did not take his place. Jesus Christ is God himself, and Jesus Christ is continuing his work on earth. The church does not, in the most important sense, become his successor. Instead, the church is united to him. This is what it means to be united to an ascended Jesus Christ, then. It means that we have received his anointing, his equipping, his Holy Spirit to do the work he calls us to now.

Being united to an ascended Jesus Christ means both of these things: our prayers go up, and the power of God comes down. Our prayers ascend to God the Father clothed in the righteousness of Jesus Christ, and the power of God the Father descends to us equipping us for life according to the righteousness of Jesus Christ. Louis Berkhof has a fantastic formulation that sums this up: "Christ pleads our cause with God, while the Holy Spirit pleads God's cause with us."[6] This is how we have been raised with him in the heavenly realms.

---

6. Berkhof, *Systematic Theology*, 301.

The Ascension of Jesus

Mission in Union with the Ascended Christ

Union with an ascended Jesus Christ equips us for our missional work. Those two consequences of union with an ascended Christ give us exactly what some in my congregation were looking for as we talked with that representative from that charity: confidence. We can engage in our mission in the world confidently as Christians because our prayers go up, and God's power comes down.

Sometimes finding this confidence is spoken of in terms of "finding your place in God's story."[7] This language is especially meaningful for young adults making their way through graduations, choosing a career, finding a place to live, partnering with another person for life. It's also meaningful for people at any age who are contemplating another upset in life—moving to a new city, finding a new job, or beginning retirement: "What is my place in God's story?"

Missiologist Christopher Wright is one who argues that in order to engage well in the mission of God we need to know the outlines of God's story. We need to know what God is up to so that we can find our place in it. Wright describes this story using the common four-part *creation-fall-redemption-new creation* rubric: God created the world good. Human beings, using the freedom God gave them, introduced sin and evil into the world in the fall. Since the Garden of Eden, through the Old Testament patriarchs, the prophets and kings, and finally perfectly in Jesus Christ, God has been redeeming his whole creation. One day, God promises to finish all this with the new creation at the time of the return of Jesus Christ.[8] That's the Bible's story. Every part of the Bible fits into that story. The better we know that story, the better we will be able to be missional—finding our place in the story.

We do need to know the story, but I think we often need something more than that. We need something more because, for much of our lives, we're not looking to "find our place." We're not graduating, moving, changing jobs, getting married, or retiring in the next few years, as far as we know. We already have a place, and we need to have confidence that our current place has something to do with God's story. And even if we know the story of God's mission well and can easily imagine how our place might

---

7. VanGelder and Zscheile, *Missional Church in Perspective*, 135–36; Roxburgh, *Missional*.

8. Wright, *Mission of God*, 35–47.

fit into that story, we might still lack confidence. We might lack the confidence that our place matters in God's mission. Does God really care about where I am? We might lack the confidence that our work can have any kind of impact. Who am I to do something for the mission of God? We need confidence that God cares about where we are and that our work really will be meaningful. That's where the ascension comes in. The ascension is about confidence for our engagement in the mission of God and his church.

The mission of the church is often associated with the ascension in the Bible. Many of the classic mission texts occur in the narrative of the life of Jesus just as he is about to ascend and send his Holy Spirit (Matt 28:20; Acts 1:8; John 20:21–22; and in the dubious longer ending of Mark). Ephesians 4:7–16, a kind of missional text, situates this mission within the context of the ascension of Jesus and the outpouring of the Holy Spirit. In these ways, the Bible teaches us to go to the doctrine of the ascension and the person of the ascended Jesus Christ to get this confidence for our mission. That confidence comes to us precisely because, through union with Jesus Christ, our prayers go up, and God's power comes down.

Missional Prayers

We need not just the prayer-confidence that God hears our prayers, but the missional confidence that God cares about our tiny place in the world—the things we pray about for ourselves and for others. One of our greatest mistakes when we pray is asking *only* "for everything we need, spiritually and physically."[9] We also need to pray for everything *others* need. Our prayers need to be a part of our mission and God's mission and not just part of our personal lives. When prayer is part of that mission, then our confidence in prayer becomes confidence in mission.

God shows us this through the letters of Paul. He writes this: "I urge, then, first of all, that petitions, prayers, intercession, and thanksgiving be made for all people" (1 Tim 2:1). When we pray, we need to ask for everything *the world* needs, spiritually and physically. The model prayer of Jesus teaches us this. We don't say, "Father in heaven, hallowed be your name. Give us our daily bread . . . ." Before we pray for our daily bread, for the things we need, we pray for God's kingdom to come and for God's will to be done. We pray for the needs of the world before we pray for our needs. God teaches us to pray missional prayers—to make prayer part of our mission.

9. "Heidelberg Catechism," Q&A 118.

Wright catalogs different kinds of missional prayers: In both the Old and New Testaments, God tells his people to pray for blessings for the nations and powers around them. The book of Daniel also shows the key role that prayer plays in confronting the powers in the world. Prayer is part of both sides of our mission with respect to authorities in the world—we pray both for them and also in opposition to their idolatrous claims. Prayer is a part of mission in the teaching of Jesus and the work of the church as reported in the book of Acts and the letters of Paul. Paul, for example, frequently reports on how he prays for the churches he writes to, and he describes prayers for one another as "help" (2 Cor 1:11). In Ephesians 6, Paul presents prayer as a key component of spiritual warfare and the mission of the church. In these ways, prayer is not an activity separate from mission. Prayer is part of mission.[10]

It is important to recognize the role of lament as a missional form of prayer. Philosopher Nicholas Wolterstorff notes that many of us feel like God is absent when we suffer. To suffer is, it often seems, to be apart from God. This is not just true when we are suffering as the result of God's anger with us. Even when, or especially when, we are suffering as victims, it can seem that God is not present. We need to pray prayers of lament because through these prayers, we gain the assurance that God is with us in our suffering.[11] This is especially important for the church's mission in the world. A major part of our mission will involve suffering with others, and a major part of our mission *must* involve crying out to God in lament on behalf of our neighbors who are suffering. The ascension of Jesus Christ gives us the confidence to do this. Because Jesus Christ, a human like us, is in heaven interceding for us, prayers of lament in union with an ascended Jesus Christ are confident prayers. In Jesus Christ, our God hears us and even suffers with us.

Consider again the anxiety we have about whether God cares about our place in his mission. I might care about the cause in front of me, but does God care? I might be grieved by the suffering the world around me, but where is God? Is this really *his* mission, or is it just my passion? This anxiety about our missional place is a cousin of the kind of anxiety that undercuts prayer. Our prayers are undercut when we approach God with anxiety—about whether he will hear us and answer.[12] For this kind of

---

10. Wright, *Mission of God*, 254–61.
11. Woltersdorff, "Liturgy and Lament."
12. Calvin, *Institutes*, III.xx.21.

anxiety, the ascension is the only solution. The ascension changes anxiety into confidence, both prayer-confidence and missional confidence. Because we are united to an ascended Jesus Christ, we are confident that our prayers are heard by God and that our human feelings about the world around us are felt by God. Our prayers go up to heaven and, inasmuch as prayer is part of mission, our place in the world rises to become a part of God's mission. Through union with an ascended Christ, we have confidence in our mission because we have confidence in all our prayers.

Missional Work

To engage in our mission, we also need confidence that our hard work can contribute in some way to God's mission. Our anxiety about this is also transformed into confidence through union with an ascended Jesus Christ. The ascension gives us confidence that we are equipped for the church's mission. That can be a new way of thinking. In the past, many thought of the mission of the church as something that certain people (missionaries) did in a faraway place (a mission field).[13] More recently, the mission of the church has been understood as something that the whole church does—all of us—wherever God sends us in our ordinary lives. In this understanding, the role of church leadership is not to do the work of the church's mission, but to equip the congregation for that mission.[14] It's not so much that missionaries do mission work, but that church leaders cultivate every believer's participation in Christ's mission. The work of the church's mission is not concentrated in just a few people but is distributed among all the members of the church. Pastor Timothy Keller puts it this way: "the whole church is in mission; every Christian is in mission" and the church needs to "equip and send the laity into the world to minister."[15]

I'm not sure that teaching this theology to my congregation would help to give them confidence. I'm a little bit afraid that if I told them they could engage in the mission of God because *I* was going to equip them, they'd look me up and down and only get more anxious! The good news is that my ordination and seminary training is not, ultimately, the source of confidence for the church's mission. *The ascension* is the source of this confidence. Through faith in Jesus Christ, we are united to an ascended

---

13. Kreider and Kreider, *Worship and Mission*, 37.

14. Van Gelder and Zscheile, *Missional Church in Perspective*, 155–57; Hirsch and Catchim, *Permanent Revolution*, 3–26.

15. Keller, *Center Church*, 259.

The Ascension of Jesus

Savior who pours out his Holy Spirit on all his members. That Spirit equips us for the church's missional work according to the gifts he has given us.

One of the most basic forms of anxiety about our missional work is the anxiety about whether we're engaging in the secular world the right way. Some of us, myself included, hear the call to ordained ministry. For others of us, whether in our main vocation or our other pursuits in life, we hear a call to do good work in the secular world. Our anxiety builds right away when we notice other Christians talking about their work in the secular world in very different ways. Am I even approaching my work the right way as a Christian?

In the next chapter, we will have the opportunity to explore some of the different models for Christian cultural engagement. Some will want to set up alternative, Christian institutions in society. Others will hear a call to work within the secular world in an explicitly Christian way. Still others will have this sense that, for the most part, there won't be much of a difference between doing good work in the secular world and doing work in the secular world as Christians. To them, being a Christian plumber is going to look an awful lot like simply begin an excellent plumber. There are a variety of approaches.[16] After Keller surveys the various models of Christian cultural engagement, he doesn't advise that one is correct and the others are false. Instead he points out that each of us has an approach to that engagement that is part of who we are in Christ; an approach to cultural engagement is part of the gifting that Jesus Christ has poured out on us by his Holy Spirit. We should learn how to inhabit that model well.[17]

As we are sent out into the world to engage in the mission of God and his church, union with an ascended Jesus Christ gives us confidence. Even at the most basic level—our model for engaging with the world as Christians—we have been equipped with specific gifts by the Holy Spirit that our ascended Jesus Christ pours out on us. With confidence, we should learn how to engage according to that model well. We are also given other gifts by the Holy Spirit. With confidence, we should learn how to use those gifts well. Through our union with an ascended Jesus Christ who pours out his Holy Spirit on us, our anxiety is replaced with confidence.

Walter C. Hobbs has collected stories of some churches that have engaged in mission with this kind of confidence—a confidence in prayer and confident reliance on the Holy Spirit. He tells of one congregation that had an opportunity to witness in their community—but it was an expensive

---

16. Tim Keller helpfully systematizes these approaches in *Center Church*, 230-32.
17. Keller, *Center Church*, 240.

opportunity. The church council told the team: "Do it." They relied on God the Holy Spirit in prayer, and they were given the means to do it. Through prayer and through depending on the Holy Spirit, they had missional confidence. In another congregation, one member felt a call to take a job at an urban school. If he took the job, it might open up opportunities for the whole church to get involved in that school. The pay was not very good, however. Through prayer and depending on the Holy Spirit, this congregation gathered around this man in missional confidence.[18] Hobbs doesn't make the connection, but this confidence in prayer and confidence in the Holy Spirit's provision which yields confidence in mission—it all comes from the union these believers have with an ascended Jesus Christ. Through that union, they have confidence that he takes their prayers to his and their Father and that he pours out his Holy Spirit on them. Through that union, their anxiety melts away into missional confidence.

Missional Liturgy for Ascension and Pentecost

Our union with our ascended Jesus Christ is supposed to be a source of missional confidence. It's supposed to take away our anxiety. We're supposed to be certain that whatever we encounter and experience out in the world, when we go to God in prayer, Jesus Christ intercedes for us, wrapping our prayers and God's hearing of them in God's own human identification with our experience. We're supposed to be assured that whatever task is placed before us, we do it by the power of God given to us as Jesus Christ sends us his Holy Spirit. We're supposed to have that confidence as a matter of habit. So where do we learn this habit?

I could hope that simply through reading this chapter, you will have learned the habit of confidence and won't have to worry about missional anxiety again. Unfortunately for both of us, human beings don't usually work like that. Placing certain beliefs in our heads doesn't automatically yield life-long emotional and behavioral change. All of us need to learn this confidence as a *habit*, and this can happen through worship. This is a point that James K. A. Smith makes more broadly about all of Christian formation: we learn it not just through ideas in our minds but even more through liturgy.[19] For missional confidence, we have a season each year when liturgy can teach us especially that. It is the time in May and June when we

---

18. Hobbs, "Dependence," 120.
19. Smith, *Imagining the Kingdom*, 3–4.

celebrate Ascension and Pentecost. Here are a few ways in which Ascension and Pentecost liturgies can help worshipers learn this habit.

Praise

One Pentecost Sunday, we began our opening liturgy of praise like this: First, the call to worship included selections from Psalms 104 through 106, describing the comprehensive work of God (and quoting 104:30, of course, since it was Pentecost after all: "When you send your Spirit, they are created . . ."). Then, I encouraged the congregation to think about all the things we had seen God do over the last week, even if we didn't notice that it was God the Holy Spirit at work at the time. I said, "Your ascended Savior has sent his Spirit to do that work." Finally, we sang "Creator, Spirit, By Whose Aid." The lyrics transition from marking the comprehensive work of God to praying that the Holy Spirit would empower us for worship and for life.

Liturgies of praise that highlight God's work in our world help us learn our place in God's story. Pastor Mike Cosper contrasts these sorts of liturgies with praise that tends to focus on the church's activity and the intensity of our singing and praising.[20] When our praise draws our attention to *God's* work, we learn to see God at work in our world and even in our lives. Alan and Eleanor Kreider also describe our opening praise in terms of God's work in our lives: "When we gather to worship God, we offer our praises out of the stories that have shaped us."[21] Ruth A. Meyers suggests beginning worship with a prayer that acknowledges the variety of places and experiences worshipers have had during the week.[22] Especially during the celebrations of Ascension and Pentecost, these praises and prayers can make reference to the ascended Lord Jesus pouring out his Holy Spirit. Liturgies like this can teach us the habit of seeing our stories as theological stories—God has been at work. Even more, we learn the habit of seeing our stories as christological and pneumatological stories—God has been at work in and around us through Jesus Christ and the Holy Spirit. Most specifically, we learn the habit of seeing our stories as Ascension and Pentecost stories—God has been at work in our lives because Jesus Christ is reigning in heaven and present with us, protecting and equipping us, having sent his Holy Spirit to us. The more our praise directs our attention to those things,

---

20. Cosper, *Rhythms of Grace*, 129.
21. Kreider and Kreider, *Worship and Mission*, 153.
22. Meyers, *Missional Worship*, 47, 72.

the more we will learn the habit of inhabiting the world as people who have the Holy Spirit.

Prayers

Our prayers can also help us learn the habit of missional confidence in union with an ascended Jesus Christ. We should pray for the world in our worship. This is one of the most common recommendations for worship leaders who want their worship to be more connected to the mission of God.[23] If we went back and listened to recordings of our worship and recorded the amount of time each element of the liturgy took, how many of us would be embarrassed to see how little we prayed? Even worse, if we also counted the minutes we spent praying about various topics, how few would we find had been devoted to prayers *for the world*? It's easy for our prayers, even in worship, to be dominated by the immediate concerns of worshipers and their sick and suffering family members. Why aren't we praying for the world in our worship?

I stumbled into the practice of praying prayers that had a heavy emphasis on the concerns of the world. When I was in seminary, I had the opportunity to preach at a variety of churches. The school maintained a schedule of local preaching opportunities, and all a student had to do was send an email to get scheduled for a particular church on a particular Sunday. Often, the congregation expected the seminarian to lead the whole liturgy, including the prayers. Typically, I knew nothing about the church until I showed up an hour before worship. When it was time to pray the "congregational prayer," I would throw in a local request or two that an elder shared with me before worship, but mostly I prayed for the world—I had to fill the prayer with something! A day or so earlier, I'd read the day's news, imagine how worshipers might be thinking about those news stories, and I'd write out prayers. Worshipers told me they appreciated my prayers. This became some of the first and most consistent feedback I received, and I've tried to continue praying like this. A few times my prayers have drifted away from "straight from the headlines" petitions for a matter of weeks. And each time, I've been asked why I quit doing it.

---

23. For example: Sunquist, *Understanding*, 299; Davies, *Worship and Mission*, 114–25; Smith, *Desiring the Kingdom*, 193–94; Tizon, *Missional Preaching*, 29; Schmit, *Sent and Gathered*, 186–87; Meyers, *Missional Worship*, 108–27.

When we regularly pray for the world, we learn the habit of living in the world in prayer. We learn the habit of expecting that God, through the intercession of the very human Jesus Christ, experiences the world as we do—in frustration, in pain, in hope, in joy. We learn confidence in our world as the people of God, because we are united to an ascended Jesus Christ, interceding and sending his Holy Spirit.

Sending

The sending liturgy at the conclusion of worship is another opportunity. The charge and benediction are more than just the conclusion of the liturgy. They ought to contain more than just a summons to get involved in some weekday church program or to return next week. The sending liturgy is perhaps the most important liturgical point of connection between gathered worship and the rest of our lives.[24] Some classic benedictions are trinitarian,[25] and some biblical blessings include reference to the Holy Spirit (Rom 15:13; 2 Cor 13:14). Benedictions like these could be introduced with a simple Ascension- and Pentecost-themed formula: "As the ascended Lord Jesus poured out his Holy Spirit on the church on the day of Pentecost, so he sends you out with his Holy Spirit . . . ."

Material Objects

Even the objects used in liturgy can teach us confidence for our part in God's story through union with an ascended Jesus Christ. Anxiety about our place and the value of our work is a material struggle. It's a struggle that takes place on pavement and soil, in flesh and blood, and with objects and forces. We're not sure if our physical location is where we're supposed to be. We're not sure if the forces we're applying to this material world are meaningful. The grace and work of God seems to be something so spiritual and invisible, and it can be hard to learn the habit of seeing the material and visible world as a place that God cares about and a place where God is working.

I wonder if we would have this same anxiety if Jesus Christ were standing next to us, working with us. Mary might have had this anxiety

---

24. Schmit, *Sent and Gathered*, 43–55; Cosper, *Rhythms of Grace*, 148–49; Smith, *Desiring the Kingdom*, 205–7.

25. Cosper, *Rhythms of Grace*, 148–49.

mixed in with her other emotions as she first heard Jesus speaking to her on the morning of the resurrection, but when she saw and recognized Jesus, everything changed. Her response would seem to leave little room for anxiety, at least in that moment (John 20:14–16). Perhaps everything would change for us if only Jesus were standing next to us—if only we knew that this material world was not the arena of his absence.

God does not want us to experience his absence in this material world. God wants us to see a connection between the material world and his ongoing work. God uses the material world again and again to assure his people that he is at work—the natural rainbow that he showed Noah; the natural stars that he showed Abram; the natural elements of the Passover that he showed to generations of Israelites. In our worship, God does the same for us.

The décor in our buildings can help us learn that confidence that comes through union with an ascended Jesus Christ. For example, if the church entrance features photographs of regular worshipers doing their regular work,[26] worshipers are reminded that what happens in the sanctuary doesn't stay in the sanctuary. They learn to be confident that Jesus Christ has something to do with their ordinary lives because they go out as people who have a Savior who is in heaven, and in their ordinary work they are united to him and he pours out his Holy Spirit to equip them for that work.

The elements of the Lord's Supper, these visible material objects through which God communicates an invisible grace, might be an almost perfect liturgical place to learn the habit of missional confidence through union with an ascended Jesus Christ. The theology of Holy Communion has been an occasion to answer our question about whether a Savior who has materially departed in his ascension can really be present with us and us with him:

> Jesus Christ remains always seated at the right hand of God the Father in heaven—but he never refrains on that account to communicate himself to us through faith. This banquet is a spiritual table at which Christ communicates himself to us with all his benefits. At that table he makes us enjoy himself as much as the merits of his suffering and death, as he nourishes, strengthens, and comforts our poor, desolate souls by the eating of his flesh, and relieves and renews them by the drinking of his blood.[27]

26. Hudson, *Imagine Church*, 99–100.
27. "Belgic Confession," Article 35; Calvin, "Calvin's Catechism (1545)," 517.

The Ascension of Jesus

The question of the presence of the ascended Jesus Christ at the Supper is one of the famous points of disagreement in the Christian tradition. We can, however, agree about this: our theology of the Lord's Supper should not give us anxiety about whether God cares about our place in the world and is at work among us. Whatever our theology, we should have confidence.

The same is true of our liturgies. As much as our theologies of the Lord's Supper can be occasions to answer our questions, our liturgies of the Lord's Supper can be occasions to address our anxieties. During the celebration of the sacrament, we can emphasize our union with the ascended Jesus Christ, as in the *sursum corda*—"Lift up your hearts"—to which the people reply—"We lift them to the Lord." With these words we learn to have confidence that God cares about where we are because we are united to an ascended Jesus Christ. At the same time, we can emphasize the naturalness of the elements and learn that God chooses to be involved in the material world through his Spirit. In fact, the bread and the wine aren't just natural elements, they are the simple products of human industry—and God has chosen to use them for a holy purpose![28] Emphasizing our union with the ascended Jesus Christ and God's choice to use even the fruits of our labor for his holy purposes can help us to learn confidence that God cares about our ordinary physical world and that he is at work in it.

For some time, I've personally baked our congregation's communion bread in my kitchen on Sunday morning. I cut the bread into small pieces, and there will be some oddly-shaped bits left behind. Occasionally, my four-year-old daughter asks to eat those leftovers. I always let her, and the illusion that God doesn't care and isn't involved in my little place in the physical world breaks every time. This bread is so ordinary that my daughter wants to snack on it before breakfast. On the other hand, in a couple of hours that same bread will be used for the most holy of purposes by the power of the Holy Spirit. Because I belong to Jesus Christ who is in heaven and because he pours out his Holy Spirit, my place and my work matter in God's holy mission.

---

28. Meyers, *Missional Worship*, 164–65, 175; Davies, *Worship and Mission*, 100; Smith, *Desiring the Kingdom*, 199–200; Bevans and Schoeder, *Constants in Context*, 363.

six

The Return of Jesus

About a week before our basement carpeting was scheduled to be replaced, I walked briskly across the room with a cup of coffee. The coffee sloshed back and forth. Then it splashed over the edge two or three times, dripped down the side of the mug, and spilled on the carpet. I kept walking nonchalantly. I'm not sure if I should admit that I took a little bit of pleasure in that. Should I admit that I even let it spill on purpose? I knew the carpeting was going to be replaced soon, so there was no sense in taking care of it. In fact, quite the opposite. I might as well enjoy the freedom to stain the carpet. There's probably something perverse, maybe even childish about that joy. It might even be sinful. After all, I'm taking joy in ruining something. Maybe that is okay when the thing being ruined is badly-worn thirty-year-old basement carpeting. But it is not okay when the thing being ruined is God's creation in general.

As Christians, we shouldn't take pleasure in the destruction of creation, even though what was true of my carpeting—that it was about to be replaced—is in a certain way true of creation. Jesus Christ is returning with his perfect kingdom. The life to come will be different from this life in all the ways it ought to be. Where there is evil now, there will be good then. Where there is decay now, there will be flourishing then. God says of his work at the return of Christ: "I am making *everything* new!" (Rev 21:5, emphasis added). That all might sound like a reason for Christians to trash this world, but it isn't. Somehow, being united to Jesus Christ who promised this all-transforming return doesn't result coffee-spilling all over the world's carpet. Why not? That's what this chapter will explore, and that's what our liturgies during the season of Advent can help to teach us.

The Return of Jesus

When the word "advent" is used in American English today, it often refers to changes in technology or culture: the advent of agriculture in human society, the advent of television, the advent of artificial intelligence or autonomous cars. The church season of Advent is about the greatest change to our world: the arrival of Jesus Christ. Advent is actually a longing for *three* arrivals of Jesus Christ: the coming of Jesus Christ in human flesh in Bethlehem, the coming of Jesus Christ into our hearts by the Holy Spirit, and the coming of Jesus Christ to bring his eternal kingdom in fullness.[1] Other chapters in this book consider those first two arrivals. The first chapter explores the coming of Jesus Christ in human flesh. The fifth chapter explores the coming of Jesus Christ into our lives by his Holy Spirit. This chapter focuses on the last coming. Jesus Christ is coming to bring his kingdom in its fullness. This is the one arrival that is still in the future for all of us, and that's why this chapter on Advent, the first season of the church year, should come at the end of this book. This is the one piece of the life and work of Jesus Christ that has not yet been completed.

United to the Returning Christ

Each of the earlier chapters in this book show that union with Christ has something specific to do with the phase of Christ's ministry celebrated in that season. Theologian Lewis Smedes shows that some theologians will describe union with Christ as a concept that has mostly to do with Christ's incarnation, or mostly to do with his suffering in our place. Smedes, however, is convinced that union with Christ, as the idea is used in the New Testament, is primarily eschatological. It especially has to do with the "last things" and the return of Christ. Union with Christ is especially about Advent, according to Smedes. It is about being transferred into membership in the kingdom of Jesus Christ, under his lordship, into a "new situation." This, he argues, is most consistent with Paul's use of the phrase "union with Christ": "Being in Christ, then, is to be within the *rule* of Christ, and within the liberating domination of the Spirit."[2] This "new situation" defines our identity in the world.

What is your identity in the world? Where I grew up, about one in every eight people belonged to my denomination, the Christian Reformed Church in North America (CRC). I learned that my religious identity was

---

1. Gross, *Living the Christian Year*, 38–39.
2. Smedes, *Union with Christ*, 65–67.

my denomination. That didn't translate when I moved to a different part of the United States. In the country at large, only one out of every 1,500 people belongs to the CRC, so it's no longer very helpful in social settings to think of myself as a "Christian Reformed" person. I could think of myself as "Reformed" more broadly, but even this often requires explanation. If someone asks about my religious identity, and I tell them I'm "Reformed," I'll often find myself first giving a lesson in church history and comparative Christian theological traditions. It's not a great way to start a conversation about Jesus. Instead, I have learned to think of myself first of all as someone who belongs to Jesus Christ. Union with Christ gives me my primary identity. It does this partly because the Christ to whom I'm united promises to return, and in this promise he tells me two things: one about myself and one about the sin and evil I struggle with every day.

What about Myself?

To be united to the returning Jesus Christ is to be a member of his coming kingdom more than I am a member of the present age. I am a foreigner and stranger here. This biblical theme extends all the way back to the story of Abram: "Go from your country, your people and your father's household to the land I will show you" (Gen 12:1). Abraham became a person looking for a better country (Heb 11:9–10). It is a lesson that the Israelites learned: "you were foreigners in Egypt" (Exod 22:21; 23:9; Lev 19:34; Deut 10:19). We who belong to the returning Christ share this identity: we are foreigners and strangers (Heb 11:13; 1 Pet 2:11). Paul puts it this way: "You are all children of the light and children of the day. We do not belong to the night or to the darkness" (1 Thess 5:5). Paul goes on to describe the radical difference this makes in the way a person lives. "Day" in this verse isn't merely a light-related metaphor for the kingdom. "Day" seems connected to the "Day of the Lord" which Paul writes about in the verses immediately preceding. Belonging to Jesus Christ is a matter of belonging to the day of his return. That is my I identity if I am united to Christ. I am a child of the future. I am a child of the coming day and daylight more than I am a child of the current age and darkness.

Many of us need to have a stronger sense of our identity as children of the future. I've needed to learn not to think of myself first of all as a child of the Christian Reformed Church. I've needed to replace that with an understanding that I am a child of the future—of the coming kingdom

The Return of Jesus

of the returning King. Some of us who grew up in one place and now live in another think of ourselves first of all as "transplants from New Jersey," or whatever. We need to replace that with an understanding that we are children of the Day of the Lord. Those of us who are older can have this sense that the world has passed us by. We come from an older time. Sometimes we can't even figure out how to have the same conversation that younger people are having. But we can't think we belong to the past. Quite the opposite. Even we need to know that first of all we belong to the future. We are united to the returning Christ and belong to his coming kingdom. That's what it means to have union with him.

How do we learn this identity? Belonging to the coming kingdom of the returning Christ is something that happens through repentance and faith. Any long discussion of the kingdom of God *has* to include this point. "If the kingdom of God is all it's cracked up to be in Scripture . . . then it's hugely important to be clear about how one gets *in* it."[3] We get into the kingdom of God through union with the King, the Christ who has promised to return, by repenting of our sins and putting our faith in him. The kingdom of God is about repentance and faith. This point is not made often enough,[4] but it needs to be made more because union with Christ through repentance and faith is what makes the return of Christ something wonderful and not terrifying.

We don't automatically belong to the kingdom of God. When we first hear these warnings by Jesus, he wants us to tremble a bit:

> Then I will tell them plainly, "I never knew you. Away from me, you evildoers!" (Matt 7:23)

> Then he will say to those on his left, "Depart me from, you who are cursed, into the eternal fire prepared for the devil and his angels." (Matt 25:41)

The return of Jesus means that judgment is coming for evildoers, and an end is coming to their evil. That needs to be terrifying before it is comforting. It needs to be terrifying first so that we flee to Christ, so that through union with him our names are written in the book of life (Rev 3:5). Then, when judgment day comes as Christ returns to bring his kingdom, our eternal home will not be determined by what we have done, but by

---

3. De Young and Gilbert, *What is the Mission*, 135.
4. Bolt, "Just What," 259–82.

what Christ has done because our names are included in the book of life (Rev 20:12). Union with a returning Christ means confidence that when the day of the Lord comes, we will be counted as members of his kingdom. In fact, it means that we count ourselves as members of that kingdom even now.

What about Evil?

Union with Christ teaches us something about the sin and evil we struggle with every day. It even affects our habits. We see the world in different ways. I turned on the radio once to hear live audio from the funeral of a police officer who had been shot and killed while performing his duties in a nearby city. His funeral had become a major event. As I tuned in, I heard the former police chief giving a eulogy. He reassured the grieving and shaken city: there might be a few bad people in the city, but most of the people are good people. I coughed and shouted out some outburst. I'm sure I would have had a different response had I been physically in attendance at the funeral. But from the distance and isolation of my home and its radio, I couldn't help arguing out loud with the theology. The world is not filled with mostly good people and a few bad people. That is not what the Bible teaches, and that's not what I believe. God tells us a different story in the Bible: "There is no one righteous, not even one . . . for all have sinned and fall short of the glory of God" (Rom 3:10, 23).

It is understandable, however, that a person would say this. Many of us were trained to believe in good guys and bad guys as kids. It's the standard worldview of fairy tales, kids' movies and cartoons, and cops-and-robbers games. The world is black-and-white, perhaps with a host of innocent bystanders. It's even understandable that a person who knows better would think that way. We have a hard time purging from our minds that Manichean worldview that insists on good guys and bad guys. It is so useful to sort the world into good guys and bad guys, and to put on black-and-white glasses as we look at the world around us. How else can we navigate through life if we can't divide what we find into good and evil, righteous and unrighteous, trustworthy and untrustworthy? The biblical perspective, which insists on seeing sin and sinners in everything, makes us unable to evaluate anything in the world, doesn't it?

It shouldn't. In union with a Christ who promises to return, I learn to evaluate the world in light of that return. Evaluating the world isn't so much a matter of trying to sort people and things into right and wrong as much as it is matter of imagining what the return of Christ will mean for everything and everyone I encounter. To help us with this imagination, Missiologist Christopher J. Wright points to the Old Testament Year of Jubilee.[5] God told the Israelites to practice the Year of Jubilee regularly so that they would learn the habit of evaluating their world in light of the future. When Joshua led the Israelites into the land of Canaan, it had been divided up, and allotments were granted to each of the tribes. Within each of the tribal allotments, specific plots were given to each family, but over time the plots didn't tend to stay in the same family. Land was sold because of debt; properties were divided because of inheritances. Some families accumulated more and more land. Other families found themselves with less and less. Those who have played the board game "Settlers of Catan" perhaps have a sense of the frustrating hopelessness that losing families might have felt. The game goes on and on and at a certain point there's no hope in winning it anymore. As one of the disadvantaged players, you can see this is the case, but you've still got to play the game out to the end. And playing the game out to the end can take a long time.

The year of Jubilee was designed to reverse the inequality and reset the map, returning the land equitably to each family. God's basic concern was his sovereignty (Psalm 24:1: "The earth is the LORD's, and everything in it"). His concern was also about opportunities for families and the effects of crippling debt. In a society where inheritance was at the heart of generational family structures, debt has long-term, nearly irreversible effects. The Jubilee could reverse that damage.[6] The Jubilee was designed to teach faith in God—the sovereignty, providence, redeeming work, forgiveness, and promises of God.[7] If you know that there will be a day when everything will be set right, you evaluate what is happening around you differently.

Jesus Christ has promised to return as a king with his perfect kingdom. His kingship over a perfect kingdom is a matter of who he is: "The Son is the image of the invisible God, the firstborn over all creation. For in him all things were created: things in heaven and on earth, visible and invisible, whether thrones or powers or rulers or authorities; all things have been created through him and for him" (Col 1:15–16). His kingship over a perfect kingdom is also a matter of action—it's a matter of what he has done

---

5. Wright, *Mission of God*, 296–97.
6. Ibid., 297–98.
7. Ibid., 299.

and will do. We look forward to our own bodily resurrection as the day when the last enemy is destroyed, and we will see this fulfillment:

> [S]o in Christ all will be made alive. But each in turn: Christ, the firstfruits; then, when he comes, those who belong to him. Then the end will come, when he hands over the kingdom to God the Father after he has destroyed all dominion, authority, and power. For he must reign until he has put all his enemies under his feet. The last enemy to be destroyed is death. (1 Cor 15:22–26)

Jesus is our King because of his very identity. He assures us of this at his baptism and throughout his peripatetic ministry.[8] Jesus is our King because he has won the victory. This is proclaimed to the world in his resurrection, celebrated at Easter.[9] But Jesus still must bring us his perfect kingdom. The enemies have been defeated, but they must be destroyed. His kingdom is perfect, but we still need to be welcomed into it. And he will do all that. This is what he assures us of during the season of Advent. To belong to him by faith is to anticipate that kingdom . . . and to use that anticipation to understand the nature of the world in this life. It's not so much a matter of dividing the world into good guys and bad guys, black and white, but more a matter of knowing with confidence that what is good will be made perfect, and what is evil will be finally done away with. That's the habit we learn in union with Christ.

Missional Union with a Returning Christ

Anyone who has Christian friends and acquaintances from diverse traditions knows how perplexing it can be to encounter a sincere Christian who approaches the world very differently. *But, shouldn't a Christian go out into the world the way I do?* we ask ourselves. These differences can be perplexing. They can be enlightening. Honestly, they can also be irritating. Some Christians are convinced that they need to withdraw from the dangerous influences in the world in order to raise their children right. Others are happy to head right out into that world, spending much of their time working on projects for the common good, even in settings where talking about Jesus Christ is difficult, if not shunned. Others charge out into the world boldly praying against demons and doing street evangelism. Then there are

---

8. See chapter 2.
9. See chapter 4.

the Christians who aggressively establish Christian schools and Christian businesses, and make Christian music. Still others are happy to quietly live their Christian lives without drawing much attention to themselves. What accounts for this variety of approaches among people who are united to the same returning Christ? Each of us is tempted to think that some of these Christians are better Christians than others. Before we fall into that conclusion, however, we should consider how these different approaches might be the consequence of the different stories the Spirit teaches us to tell ourselves in union with Christ.

Mission and Two Stories

Union with a returning Christ means that the Holy Spirit teaches us to see ourselves and to see the world in certain ways. Think of these as two stories. As we go through life, we find that we're telling ourselves a story about who we are, and we find that we are telling ourselves another story about the way the world is. But God the Holy Spirit is here to correct our stories and teach us the true stories.

That doesn't mean that the Holy Spirit teaches all of us the *same* exact stories. After all, God's grace transforms each of us at different times in our lives and in ways that are unique to the personalities he created us with and the gifts he has given us in transformation. And God has sent us out to different places in the world, seeing it from unique vantage points. I might learn from the Holy Spirit to tell a story about myself as a person who is in the thick of a deep struggle with temptations and another story about a world beset with greed and selfishness. You might learn from the Holy Spirit to tell a story about yourself as someone who is gifted to speak boldly about the gospel and a story about a world bewildered by uncertainty and a search for meaning. But if our stories differ, because our personalities, locations, gifts, and progress in sanctification differ, then our models for engaging the world should differ, too.

Pastor Timothy Keller argues that all of our varied approaches to the culture can be categorized into four basic models: relevance, two kingdoms, counterculturalist, and transformationist. Keller defines these models by the answers to two questions: "Should we be pessimistic or optimistic about the possibility for cultural change?" and "Is the current culture redeemable and good, or fundamentally fallen?"[10] The relevance model, which includes

---

10. Keller, *Center Church*, 225.

liberation theology and the seeker-sensitive movement, is defined by an optimism about changing the culture and a positive evaluation of the goodness of the culture. The two kingdoms model is defined by a pessimism about the possibility for cultural change and a generally positive evaluation of the goodness of the culture. The counterculturalist model, which includes the Anabaptist tradition, is defined by a pessimism about changing the culture and a negative evaluation of the goodness of the culture. The transformationist model is optimistic about cultural change and evaluates the culture negatively.[11] Keller argues that all of the major Christian approaches to engaging the world can be categorized as a form of one of those four models. He advises believers to avoid thinking that one is right and the others are wrong. Instead, believers should appreciate all the models, should think about which model is needed in the current environment, and should consider which model best fits their gifts and calling.[12]

The two attitudes that define each of these models—optimism about whether the world can be changed and positivity about how good the world is—are related to the two stories that union with Christ teaches us tell ourselves. Our optimism about whether we can transform the world is influenced by (but not completely determined by) the story we tell about ourselves. For some of us, this is a story about someone who is often very obviously out of place. We notice it. We feel it. We just don't fit in. One of my friends has a certain group of acquaintances who know him as "the guy who goes to church." It's not just that they know he goes to church. This has become his identity among them. Some even use it as though it is his name: "the guy who goes to church." Conversations frequently return to this point. His identity as a church-goer affects everything he does in that setting. If that's the kind of story we tell about ourselves, if we really do feel that out-of-place because of our union with a returning Christ, it's because we have a strong sense that we have been transformed, that we have the almighty Holy Spirit in us, and we are constantly struggling against the powers of evil in this world. This often goes hand-in-hand with being optimistic about the possibility that the world can be changed. After all, the only reason I feel so out of place is that *God himself*, God the Holy Spirit, is in me. Of course he can use me to change the world for the better! That's why he has placed me, someone who belongs to his perfect coming kingdom, in my place in this imperfect, suffering world. For others of us, the story we tell about

11. Keller, *Center Church*, 194–217, 230–32.
12. Ibid., 235–42.

ourselves is a story of someone who fits in all too well with the world. If the previous story drives a person to lament their isolation as a Christian in a hostile world, this story drives a person to confess their complicity in the sin and evil that characterize the world. When I'm telling myself this story, I'm likely to avoid getting too entangled with the world. I find myself with a pessimism about whether the world is really capable of being changed.

These two varieties of the story we tell about ourselves stem from a balance between the fact that Jesus describes his kingdom as something that is already here and something that is yet to come. In one sense, the kingdom of God is already here, and I belong to it. In another sense, the kingdom of God is yet to come, and I'm not yet what I will be. On the one hand, I have been transformed by Christ. On the other hand, I have yet to be transformed. As the Holy Spirit teaches us to tell a story about ourselves, we learn to weigh these two realities differently. That's how union with a returning Christ can teach some of us to be optimistic and others to be pessimistic about whether the world can be transformed.

That other attitude that defines Keller's four approaches—positivity about how good the world is—is influenced by the story we have learned to tell about the world in union with a coming Christ. That story involves a tension between the necessity of Christ's return and the nature of Christ's return. On the one hand, Christ's return is necessary. "[T]he Bible presents the public square, human life lived in society and the marketplace, as riddled with sin, corruption, greed, injustice and violence."[13] This world is not the way it is supposed to be. We will keep telling ourselves that truth as we go out into the world if we have union with a returning Christ. On the other hand, the return of Christ will not involve a complete obliteration of this world. That's because he created it good, and even the corrupting power of evil cannot completely destroy that goodness. Missiologist Christopher Wright writes about the meaning of Isaiah 65, 2 Peter 3, and Revelation 21: "All that has enriched and honoured the life of all nations in all history will be brought in to enrich the new creation. The new creation will not be a blank page, as if God will simply crumple up the whole of human historical life in this creation and toss it in the cosmic bin, and then hand us a new sheet to start all over again."[14] The nature of Christ's return will be a cleansing and purging more than a destroying and wiping out. Because Jesus Christ, when he returns, will keep some of what we see as

---

13. Wright, *Mission of God's People*, 227.
14. Ibid., 228.

he brings his kingdom, we should see some of what will be in the world around us. There is this tension between the necessity of Christ's return and the nature of Christ's return in the story the Holy Spirit teaches us to tell about the world around us. For some of us, that story will emphasize more the necessity of Christ's return and the evil that needs to be purged. For others of us, that story will emphasize more that Christ's return will involve the preservation of all that is good in this world. And it's natural that each of us would have an internal narrative that is slightly different because each of us is sent out into the world in a unique place. Our unique stories, with their unique emphases, will result in different kinds of approaches to the world. Wright writes:

> On the one hand, we are called to *constructive engagement* in the world—because it is God's world, created, loved, valued and redeemed by him. But on the other hand, we are called to *courageous confrontation* with the world—because it is a world in rebellion against God, the playground of other gods, standing under God's condemnation and ultimate judgment.[15]

A Mission of Hope

At the heart of all of these models is hope. Whether your internal narrative about yourself more emphasizes sanctification or more emphasizes the need for confession, whether in your view the world looks dim or bright, whatever model of engagement with the world you naturally adopt, if you are united to a returning Christ, hope will be at the heart of all of it.

Hope is one of the most common Advent themes, and hope is something that many of our congregations badly need. Many of us worship in places where the institutions and ideas of Christianity seem to be waning in cultural influence. Many of our older fellow worshipers tell us that they remember seeing a "Christian culture" all around, but they don't see it so much anymore. That's not just a judgment about what they see on TV and Facebook. That's a judgment about what they see in their own neighborhoods. Sociologist Rodney Stark might be correct when he notes that neither the world at large nor the United States in particular is becoming more "secular" in the dramatic way many predicted in previous centuries.[16] Nev-

---

15. Wright, *Mission of God's People*, 229.
16. Stark, *Triumph*, 369–85.

ertheless, the number of people who are committed to religious institutions is noticeably declining in many places. Christians who remember a more "Christianized" past, even if their memories exaggerate the change, need hope. Hope is also important for congregations and denominations that are experiencing steep membership declines. My own denomination enjoyed brisk membership growth almost through the end of the twentieth century. For 150 years, waves of Dutch immigration and large families resulted in one generation after another of loyal churchgoers. The immigration has stopped, the denominational loyalty has evaporated, the boom is over, and many in my denomination (and, probably, yours) need hope. And even if the culture where you live is more "Christian" than it has ever been, and your congregation or denomination is growing rapidly, you surely still need hope.

The world does not give us real and lasting reasons to hope, but union with a returning Christ does. And that is the very core of our celebration of Advent. Jesus Christ is coming with his eternal kingdom. That is who he is: a coming Christ. And we are united to him. In hope, some of us will set up alternative communities. Within a culture that organizes around the worship of false gods, some of us will organize a counterculture around the gospel of Jesus Christ. Others of us will engage more actively and integrally with the culture around us, developing strategies for doing public, gospel theology in the midst of our secular world. In places that used to be dominated by the ideas and institutions of Christianity, we will find ways to be Christian companions and partners in a post-Christian world.[17] However we do this, we do so in hope that springs from union with Christ. That hope winds its way through the stories we're learning about who we are and the way the world is.

This is why, as Christians, we don't make our way through the world spilling metaphorical coffee on the carpet. Why not? Because through union with Jesus Christ, we learn certain stories about ourselves and our world, and those stories are stories of hope. We're not just destined for a new creation, we already belong to it. Sometimes we're more confident that we can improve what we see in the world around us because we have been so transformed into people of the kingdom. So, we work for the transformative good of the world. Sometimes we're more aware that we are too easily tempted to live as though we naturally belong in this age. So, we try not to get too entangled in it. But in either case, we know that our attitude

---

17. Van Gelder and Zscheile, *Missional Church in Perspective*, 141–15.

shouldn't be that of a person who is gleefully spilling coffee on a worn-out world. That's not the kind of people we are. In union with Christ, the Holy Spirit teaches us a different story about ourselves. It's a story of hope about the people we will be in the world we are promised when Christ returns.

We also don't go spilling coffee in this world because of what we believe about the world itself. In union with Christ, we're taught a story of hope for creation—that God loves his creation and he will purify it of all that is wrong. Sometimes it is easier for us to see that this creation is *God's* creation which is destined for purification. At other times it is easier for us to see why God *needs* to purify it. But in both cases, we regard this creation as God's, and we shouldn't be eager to trash it. In union with Christ, the Holy Spirit teaches us a story about hope for this creation. That's why we treat it with care.

Missional Liturgy for Advent

Advent liturgies can be excellent opportunities for us to learn these stories of hope through union with a returning Christ. After all, Advent is all about the return of Christ. "O Come, O Come, Immanuel," is as much about the second coming as it is about the first coming. Every time our minds form those words, we are learning a story-telling habit. The lighting of Advent candles is introduced by messages of hope. As we witness the increasing light from that wreath, our eyes are learning a story-telling habit. We're learning hope, and throughout the liturgy, there are opportunities for us to learn this hope.

The Circumstances of Worship

Worship happens at a certain time, in a certain place, surrounded by certain sights and sounds. Before the liturgy even begins, the circumstances of worship can help us learn these spiritual stories of hope. One of these circumstances is the day of the week. Many of us worship regularly on Sundays, and if we were asked why, we'd might say, "because that's the way we've always done it," or, more theologically, "because that's the day when Christ rose from the dead." That's all true. However, the early church learned to see their Sunday worship as a reminder of the coming of Jesus Christ. The very fact that we worship on Sunday can help us remember that Christ is coming in hope. Sunday was called "the Lord's Day," just as the return of Christ was called "the day of the Lord." The early church identified the day of week not just as the first day, but as the eighth day. In this age, creation only enjoys seven days a week. To identify the day of worship as the eighth day is to place it in a new age, in the age to come.[18] Sunday is not just an echo of the resurrection, it is an anticipation of the coming kingdom.

- Make this connection explicit. When the congregation is called to worship or when the congregation is sent out at the end of worship, point out that the name "the Lord's Day" or the number, the eighth day, identifies this day with the coming kingdom of Jesus Christ. "Sunday is called the 'Lord's Day,' and the return of Christ is called the same thing, the 'day of the Lord.' So, let's gather again on the day of the Lord."

Music

We worship with certain music. We might hear the music of the church as we enter the worship space, and we're certainly going to hear music throughout the liturgy. The music itself can teach us a story about the world. Cultural and global music can teach us that *this* is the world Christ will cleanse when he returns. Linford L. Stutzman and George L. Hunsberger examined one church that intentionally used global music in worship. This use of music taught the congregation to make a choice between stories: are they telling a story about their identity as members of a specific nation and culture or as members of kingdom people who transcend every nation and culture?[19] In this way, the use of global music can reinforce the story a person or church tells about themselves. Local music can reinforce a story about the world, too. Stutzman and Hunsberger also argue that the use of locally-composed music proclaims that the gospel, the coming kingdom of Jesus Christ, means something for the immediate context, the world here and now.[20] Theologian John D. Witvliet describes how some churches use music and other components of worship to give worshipers an otherworldly sense. In this way, music can help us learn that our stories and the story of the world need to be about hope—about something different than what we

---

18. Meyers, *Missional Worship*, 65–66.
19. Stutzman and Hunsberger, "Public Witness," 108–9.
20. Ibid., 112–13.

see here and now.[21] Handel's *Messiah* does this for me. A Christmas tradition in our congregation is the singing of Handel's "Hallelujah" chorus. I've also begun playing recordings of the *Messiah* at home during Advent, and I've joined a local group for a *Messiah* sing-a-long each December. I love all of this because that music teaches me to long for heaven.

- Use global music during Advent to reinforce that story of hope about ourselves—that we belong to a kingdom people from every nation, tribe, people, and language who will be gathered by Christ when he returns.

- Use locally-composed music during Advent to reinforce that story of hope about our world—that this world and the products within it are not altogether evil and bound for destruction. Rather, when Christ returns, God will purify this world.

- Use beautiful, heavenly, transcendent music (whatever that means in your context) to reinforce a hopefulness in the beautiful coming kingdom of Jesus Christ.

Gathering

It isn't just the circumstances of worship that can help us to learn these stories of union with a returning Christ. The Advent liturgy itself—the things that are said and done—can help us learn these stories better and better. As we gather for worship, we learn this distinction between the world as it is and the world as it ought to be. The very act of gathering together as worshipers in Christ, usually dispersed throughout our world, reinforces that story we tell about ourselves: that though we live in the world of this age, we really belong in the coming kingdom of Jesus Christ. As we gather, we separate ourselves from those who are not gathering. The reminders of this separation are often stark: "Our neighbor's home might still be quiet and darkened; folks down the street might already be mowing their lawn; we might walk softly through the dormitory hall because many of our peers won't emerge for hours; we may even be leaving family members in our own home who don't answer this call to worship, this summons to gather."[22] (Here in Upstate New York, the lawn mowers will be replaced with snow

---

21. Witvliet, *Worship Seeking Understanding*, 105–6.
22. Smith, *Desiring the Kingdom*, 161.

blowers and snowmobiles during Advent.) Professor James K. A. Smith argues that experiencing this distinction teaches us that we are people who are "called out from among the nations."[23] But we are called out from among the nations *to* a specific place: the coming kingdom of Jesus Christ. The experience of gathering *can* help us to learn this story of hope about ourselves, that we belong to the coming kingdom of Jesus Christ, but we might need help. In fact, Smith explains that the fact of gathering can actually cut against this when we are gathering in segregated churches. The people who belong to the kingdom of Jesus Christ are worshipers "from every tribe and language and people and nation" (Rev 5:9), but most of our churches don't exactly look like that. Smith writes hopefully: "Our gathering is an act of eschatological hope that amounts to a kind of defiance . . . ."[24] Our gathering *can* be an act of defiance against the evil forces of systemic racism that keep our worship segregated even in multicultural cities, but we might need to be reminded that it is an act of defiance. It will be all too easy to learn a different story, to allow the homogeneity of our congregations to teach us that we are people of this divided world, rather than people of the coming diverse kingdom. To help worshipers learn this story of hope about themselves as they gather for worship, here are some suggestions, some ways to welcome worshipers:

- "God gathers us here this morning just as he will one day gather all of us to worship him on the day of Christ's return."
- "I hope you came here this morning eager for heaven."
- "Where did you come from this morning? As God gathers us to worship him, let's remember where we are going to in Jesus Christ."

One Advent, we went a step further in our church. Each week we had one worshiper come forward to light the Advent candle. Before they did, I asked them this question: "What is your hope this Advent season?" I had arranged with them ahead of time to answer in a way that connected with what Jesus Christ promises in his return. Then, in hope, they lit the next candle. When we together hear one person's story of who they are and how they see the world in union with a returning Christ, we can learn our own stories better, too.

---

23. Smith, *Desiring the Kingdom*, 161.
24. Ibid., 162.

Lament

A traditional liturgy often continues with confession of sin, lament, and assurance of forgiveness. This part of the liturgy during Advent also provides an opportunity to have these stories of hope reinforced. If our Advent gathering liturgy teaches us to tell that story about a people who belong to a world that is yet to come, there is a temptation to think that we need to leave all our cares at the door. After all, we don't belong to this world. Shouldn't we be unencumbered by its problems? In one sense, sure, we're not supposed to let the anxieties of life distract us from the coming kingdom of Jesus Christ (Luke 21:34). However, that doesn't mean we just try to ignore those problems and anxieties. The laments of the Bible teach us what to do: we bring these cares to God in the context of a faith that leads us to hope.[25] A lament is different than a complaint. Complaints end in uncertainty. Will anyone listen? Will anything be done? Laments end in hope. Bringing laments to God is one way to practice retelling ourselves the story of the world: that God cares about this sad world, and when Christ returns he will purify it of all that is wrong.

During Advent, laments can be offered to God in worship following the biblical pattern of lament. When we offer biblical laments, we put our painful observations about the state of the world into the context of that story of the world that the Spirit teaches us to tell in union with a returning Christ. We cry out to God, detailing the suffering of the world, asking God for his intervention, and expressing hope in God's sure response.[26] Here's an example of how this can be done. One Sunday, we brought a series of laments to God, ending each with one of the "O Antiphons" as they are found in the hymn "O Come, O Come, Emmanuel":[27]

- We lamented that so many of our friends have chosen to ignore or reject the gospel of Christ and that so many people around the world are rejected and persecuted because of the gospel. Then we prayed: "O come, O come, Immanuel, and ransom captive Israel that mourns in lonely exile here until the Son of God appear."

- We lamented the broken international relationships between warring nations and broken relationships within our own families and

---

25. Rienstra and Rienstra, *Worship Words*, 223–25.

26. Westermann, *Praise and Lament*, 170; Rienstra and Rienstra, *Worship Words*, 224–25.

27. This is an adaptation of a prayer found in *Worship Sourcebook*, 464–65.

community. Then we prayed: "O come, O King of nations, bind in one the hearts of all mankind. Bid all our sad divisions cease, and be yourself our King of peace."

- We lamented the racism that tears apart nations and communities and the abuse that harms victims. Then we prayed: "O come, O Bright and Morning Star, and bring us comfort from afar! Dispel the shadows of the night and turn our darkness into light."
- The prayer concluded with an expression of confident hope—a reading from Isaiah 11:3–9:

> He will not judge by what he sees with his eyes,
>   or decide by what he hears with his ears;
> but with righteousness he will judge the needy,
>   with justice he will give decisions for the poor of the earth.
> He will strike the earth with the rod of his mouth;
>   with the breath of his lips he will slay the wicked.
> Righteousness will be his belt
>   and faithfulness the sash around his waist.
> The wolf will live with the lamb,
>   the leopard will lie down with the goat,
> the calf and the lion and the yearling together;
>   and a little child will lead them.
> The cow will feed with the bear,
>   their young will lie down together,
>   and the lion will eat straw like the ox.
> The infant will play near the cobra's den,
>   the young child will put its hand into the viper's nest.
> They will neither harm nor destroy
>   on all my holy mountain,
> for the earth will be filled with the knowledge of the Lord
>   as the waters cover the sea.

The Lord's Supper

Worshipers can have their stories about themselves and the world reinforced during Advent celebrations of the Lord's Supper. Jesus twice uses the celebration of a meal to highlight the distinction between the world as it is and the world as it is transformed by his grace. After feeding the multitude on the hillside, Jesus explained:

> Very truly I tell you, you are looking for me, not because you saw the signs I performed but because you ate the loaves and had your fill. Do not work for food that spoils, but for food that endures to eternal life, which the Son of Man will give you. For on him God the Father has placed his seal of approval. (John 6:26–27)

This text can be read, and an invitation to eat and drink from the table can be phrased to help worshipers eat and drink as a participation in this story about themselves or about the world:

- "We often work so hard for things that are only going to spoil. Come to this table and know that Jesus Christ feeds us with his body and blood, so that we belong to a world where nothing will spoil."

Jesus also linked the sacrament of the Lord's Supper to his return when he said: "For I tell you, I will not eat it again until it finds fulfillment in the kingdom of God. . . . For I tell you I will not drink again from the fruit of the vine until the kingdom of God comes" (Luke 22:16, 18). This text, or even just its basic idea, can be used in an Advent invitation to the table:

- "You may be disappointed with who you are and what you have done. Come to this table in faith that Jesus Christ will eat and drink with you one day when he returns and fully transforms you according to his own righteousness."
- "We may be disappointed with the world. Come to this table in faith that Jesus Christ will eat and drink with us one day when he returns and transforms this world according to his glory."

Sending

As the gathered worship concludes, and worshipers prepare to scatter, even the concluding liturgy can teach them to go out telling these stories of union with a returning Christ. In fact, the sending portion of the liturgy might be the most natural place to rehearse these Advent stories. Pastor Mike Cosper suggests a corporate dedication or commitment to the mission of the church might be an appropriate way to inhabit the story of a people who belong to the coming kingdom. In fact, our union with a returning Christ ought to add a bit of urgency to go out and engage in the mission of the church (rather than spilling coffee on the carpet):

> The day is coming when Christ will return to judge the living and the dead, and the urgency of that day's approach calls us to go back into the world serious about mission and serious about living out the new identity given to us as God's people. An affirmation of faith or an affirmation of commitment is sometimes confessed together before the church is sent out.[28]

Commissioning missionaries and even ordinary people[29] to their work in the world is another way to learn these stories better—that we are people who belong to the coming kingdom and who live in a troubled world that our returning Christ promises to purify. A study of my own congregation confirmed that when worshipers see how their peers are inhabiting those stories, they begin to learn their own stories better.[30]

During the season of Advent, carefully-planned liturgies can help us learn to be people who don't go spilling coffee on the carpet. We're united to a returning Christ. Through this union, the Holy Spirit teaches us to tell certain stories about ourselves and the world, and these stories result in a variety of approaches to engaging in our mission. Liturgies that focus on hope can help us learn these stories better and better so that we go out into the world engaging in our mission in union with a Christ who has promised to return.

---

28. Cosper, *Rhythms of Grace*, 146–47.
29. Schmit, *Sent and Gathered*, 159–60; Hudson, *Imagine Church*, 100–101.
30. Monsma, "Sending Worshipers," 93–108.

Epilogue

IN SOME WAYS, THIS book has been about things at opposite ends of a spectrum. There's one gigantic thing and a host of tiny things. The gigantic thing is missional work in union with Christ, and the tiny things are the little liturgical suggestions that have concluded each chapter. Some of those liturgies seem too little—especially in comparison to union with Jesus Christ. But this is church ministry—doing tiny things that relate to a gigantic thing. Who would guess that when the disciples of Jesus announce that sins are forgiven, this would actually have to do with God's very forgiveness of sins? And yet, that is exactly what Jesus promises his disciples: "If you forgive anyone's sins, their sins are forgiven . . ." (John 20:23). The tiny words of a disciple can actually relate to the gigantic mercy of God. We can put into practice the liturgies recommended in the pages of this book in a similar hope: that our tiny practices in church ministry can actually relate to the gigantic work of God in Jesus Christ.

This book has also been about things that are hard to measure. Your liturgy during the season of Lent is now peppered with acknowledgments about the innocence of Christ, his willingness, and the efficacy of his sacrifice—all with a view toward the work that God is sending your congregation out to do. Will that make any difference? How would you know? Will you be able to see it this year, or will it take five or ten years before you notice any difference in your congregation? This is one of the things that I found disappointing about my own Doctor of Ministry research in my congregation: quite often, the things we're working on in church ministry are difficult, even impossible to measure. Of course, there are some things that are easy to measure: baptisms, conversions, church attendance. But as much of our work in church leadership is aimed at transformation, that will take a lifetime . . . and won't be complete until Jesus returns.

We need to remember the presence of the Holy Spirit. Just before Jesus said, "If you forgive anyone's sins, their sins are forgiven," he "breathed on them and said, 'Receive the Holy Spirit'" (John 20:22). That's why our tiny actions *can* relate to God's gigantic work. And we need to remember the invisibility of the Holy Spirit. The hymn "God Moves in a Mysterious Way" ought to be one of the anthems of church ministry.

The practices this book aims at might seem tiny in comparison to the theology of union with Christ, and the outcomes might be so hard to measure that you'll wonder whether they make any difference. Nevertheless, I hope you'll find worshiping in union with the Christ who equips us for our mission as thrilling as I do. Jesus Christ is with us and in us as we worship, he is with us and in us as we go out into the world, and every time we see that, in every season, we see the grace of God.

Bibliography

Barrett, Lois Y. "Taking Risks as a Contrast Community." In *Treasure in Clay Jars: Patterns in Missional Faithfulness*, edited by Lois Y. Barrett, 74–83. Grand Rapids: Eerdmans, 2004.
Bavinck, Herman. *Reformed Dogmatics*. Edited by John Bolt. Translated by John Vriend. Grand Rapids: Baker Academic, 2006.
"The Belgic Confession." In *Our Faith: Ecumenical Creeds, Reformed Confessions, and Other Resources*, 25–68. Grand Rapids: Faith Alive Christian Resources, 2013.
Benson, Bruce Ellis. *Liturgy as a Way of Life: Embodying the Arts in Christian Worship*. Grand Rapids: Baker Academic, 2013.
Berkhof, Louis. *Systematic Theology*. Grand Rapids: Eerdmans, 1996.
Bevans, Stephen B., and Roger Schroeder. *Constants in Context: A Theology of Mission for Today*. Maryknoll, NY: Orbis, 2004.
Billings, J. Todd. *Calvin, Participation, and the Gift: The Activity of Believers in Union with Christ*. Oxford: Oxford University Press, 2008.
———. *Union with Christ: Reframing Theology and Ministry for the Church*. Grand Rapids: Baker Academic, 2011.
Bolt, John. "Just What Do You Mean—Kingdom of God?" *Calvin Theological Journal* 51, no. 2 (2016) 259–82.
Bruner, Frederick Dale. *Matthew: A Commentary*. Vol. 1, *The Christbook, Matthew 1–12*. Grand Rapids: Eerdmans, 2004.
Calvin, John. "Calvin's Catechism (1537)." In *Reformed Confessions of the 16th and 17th Centuries in English Translation*. Vol. 1, *1523–1552*, 353–92. Compiled with Introductions by James T. Dennison, Jr. Grand Rapids: Reformation Heritage, 2008.
———. "Calvin's Catechism (1545)." In *Reformed Confessions of the 16th and 17th Centuries in English Translation*. Vol. 1, *1523–1552*, 467–519. Compiled with Introductions by James T. Dennison, Jr. Grand Rapids: Reformation Heritage, 2008.
———. *Institutes of the Christian Religion*. 2 vols. The Library of Christian Classics, vols. 20–21. Philadelphia: Westminster, 1960.
"The Canons of Dort." In *Our Faith: Ecumenical Creeds, Reformed Confessions, and Other Resources*, 118–44. Grand Rapids: Faith Alive Christian Resources, 2013.
Casper, Jayson. "International Forgiveness: Muslims Moved as Coptic Christians Do the Unimaginable." *Christianity Today*, April 2017. Accessed December 6, 2017. http://www.christianitytoday.com/news/2017/april/forgiveness-muslims-moved-coptic-christians-egypt-isis.html.

Bibliography

Chan, Simon. *Liturgical Theology: The Church as Worshiping Community.* Downers Grove, IL: IVP Academic, 2006.

Cosper, Mike. *Rhythms of Grace: How the Church's Worship Tells the Story of the Gospel.* Wheaton, IL: Crossway, 2013.

Crump, David. *Knocking on Heaven's Door: A New Testament Theology of Petitionary Prayer.* Grand Rapids: Baker Academic, 2006.

Davies, J. G. *Worship and Mission.* New York: Association, 1967.

DeYoung, Kevin, and Gregory D. Gilbert. *What Is the Mission of the Church? Making Sense of Social Justice, Shalom, and the Great Commission.* Wheaton, IL: Crossway, 2011.

Farrow, Douglas. *Ascension and Ecclesia: On the Significance of the Doctrine of the Ascension for Ecclesiology and Christian Cosmology.* Grand Rapids: Eerdmans, 1999.

"Form for the Lord's Supper." In *Psalter Hymnal: Doctrinal Standards and Liturgy of the Christian Reformed Church,* 90–94. Grand Rapids: Publication Committee of the Christian Reformed Church, 1934.

Frost, Michael. *The Road to Missional: Journey to the Center of the Church.* Grand Rapids: Baker, 2011.

Green, Joel B. *The Theology of the Gospel of Luke.* Cambridge: Cambridge University Press, 1995.

Gross, Bobby. *Living the Christian Year: Time to Inhabit the Story of God.* Downers Grove, IL: IVP, 2009.

"The Heidelberg Catechism." In *Our Faith: Ecumenical Creeds, Reformed Confessions, and Other Resources,* 69–117. Grand Rapids: Faith Alive Christian Resources, 2013.

Hirsch, Alan, and Tim Catchim. *The Permanent Revolution: Apostolic Imagination and Practice for the 21st Century Church.* San Francisco: Jossey-Bass, 2012.

Hobbs, Walter C. "Dependence on the Holy Spirit." In *Treasure in Clay Jars: Patterns in Missional Faithfulness,* edited by Lois Y. Barrett, 117–25. Grand Rapids: Eerdmans, 2004.

House, Renee S. "Becoming a 'Missional' Denomination for the 21st Century: A Constructive Analysis of Theology and Specific Practices in the Reformed Church in America." PhD diss., Princeton Theological Seminary, 2008.

Hudson, Neil. *Imagine Church: Releasing Whole-Life Disciples.* Nottingham, UK: IVP, 2012.

Hyde, Daniel R. "In Defense of the *Descendit*: A Confessional Response to Contemporary Critics of Christ's Descent into Hell." *The Confessional Presbyterian* 3 (2007) 104–17.

Immink, F. Gerrit. *The Touch of the Sacred: The Practice, Theology, and Tradition of Christian Worship.* Grand Rapids: Eerdmans, 2014.

Keller, Timothy J. *Center Church: Doing Balanced, Gospel-Centered Ministry in Your City.* Grand Rapids: Zondervan, 2012.

Klooster, Fred H. *Our Only Comfort: A Comprehensive Commentary on the Heidelberg Catechism.* Grand Rapids: Faith Alive Christian Resources, 2001.

Kraybill, Donald B., et al. "Amish Grace and the Rest of Us." *Christianity Today,* September, 2007. Accessed December 6, 2017. http://www.christianitytoday.com/ct/2007/septemberweb-only/138-13.0.html.

Kreider, Alan, and Eleanor Kreider. *Worship and Mission after Christendom.* Harrisonburg, VA: Herald, 2011.

Labberton, Mark. *The Dangerous Act of Worship: Living God's Call to Justice.* Downers Grove, IL: IVP, 2007.

Bibliography

"The Larger Catechism." In *Book of Confessions: Study Edition*, 247–85. Louisville, KY: Geneva, 1996.

Lathrop, Gordon W. *Holy People: A Liturgical Ecclesiology*. Minneapolis, MN: Fortress, 1999.

Lathrop, Gordon W. "Liturgy and Mission in the North American Context." In *Inside Out: Worship in an Age of Mission*, edited by Thomas H. Schattauer, 201–12. Minneapolis, MN: Fortress, 1999.

Lewis, C. S. *Perelandra*. New York: Scribner, 1972.

Mackenzie, Carine. *Stories Jesus Told: The Foolish Farmer*. Fearn, UK: Christian Focus, 2004.

Meyers, Ruth A. "Missional Church, Missional Liturgy." *Theology Today* 67, no 1 (2010) 36–50.

———. *Missional Worship, Worshipful Mission: Gathering as God's People, Going Out in God's Name*. Grand Rapids: Eerdmans, 2014.

Monsma, Nicholas W. "Pentecost and Missional Worship." *Reformed Worship* 123 (March 2017) 25–27.

———. "Sending Worshipers on a Mission: Liturgy for Missional Transformation according to Christ's Threefold Office." DMin thesis, Gordon-Conwell Theological Seminary, 2017.

Murray, John. "The Agency in Definitive Sanctification." In *The Collected Writings of John Murray*, vol. 2, 285–93. Edinburgh: Banner of Truth Trust, 2009.

Parry, Robin A. *The Biblical Cosmos: A Pilgrim's Guide to the Weird and Wonderful World of the Bible*. Eugene, OR: Cascade, 2014.

———. *Worshipping Trinity: Coming Back to the Heart of Worship*. 2nd ed. Eugene, OR: Cascade, 2012.

Psalter Hymnal. Grand Rapids: CRC, 1988.

Rienstra, Debra, and Ron Rienstra. *Worship Words: Discipling Language for Faithful Ministry*. Grand Rapids: Baker Academic, 2009.

Roxburgh, Alan J. *Missional: Joining God in the Neighborhood*. Grand Rapids: Baker, 2011.

Schattauer, Thomas H. "Liturgical Assembly as Locus of Mission." In *Inside Out: Worship in an Age of Mission*, edited by Thomas H. Schattauer, 1–21. Minneapolis, MN: Fortress, 1999.

Schmit, Clayton J. *Sent and Gathered: A Worship Manual for the Missional Church*. Grand Rapids: Baker Academic, 2009.

Schoon, Christopher James. "Missional Worship for Missional Living." Christian Reformed Church webinar, May 7, 2014. Accessed April 20, 2016. http://network.crcna.org/sites/default/files/documents/MissionalWorshipSlidesHandout.pdf.

———. "Toward a Communally Embodied Gospel: Exploring the Role of Worship in Cultivating an Evangelistic Character among God's People within the Missional Church Movement." ThD thesis, Wycliffe College and the University of Toronto, 2016.

The Service for the Lord's Day. Philadelphia: Westminster, 1984.

Sherman, Robert. *King, Priest, and Prophet: A Trinitarian Theology of Atonement*. London: T. & T. Clark, 2004.

Smedes, Lewis B. *Union with Christ: A Biblical View of the New Life in Jesus Christ*. Grand Rapids: Eerdmans, 1983.

Smith, James K. A. *Desiring the Kingdom: Worship, Worldview, and Cultural Formation*. Grand Rapids: Baker Academic, 2009.

Bibliography

———. *Imagining the Kingdom: How Worship Works.* Grand Rapids: Baker Academic, 2013.

Stark, Rodney. *The Triumph of Christianity: How the Jesus Movement Became the World's Largest Religion.* New York: HarperCollins, 2011.

Stookey, Laurence Hull. *Calendar: Christ's Time for the Church.* Nashville, TN: Abingdon, 1996.

Stutzman, Linford L., and George R. Hunsberger. "The Public Witness of Worship." In *Treasure in Clay Jars: Patterns in Missional Faithfulness,* edited by Lois Y. Barrett, 100–106. Grand Rapids: Eerdmans, 2004.

Sunquist, Scott W. *Understanding Christian Mission: Participation in Suffering and Glory.* Grand Rapids: Baker, 2013.

Tizon, Al. *Missional Preaching: Engage, Embrace, Transform.* Valley Forge, PA: Judson, 2012.

Torrance, James B. *Worship, Community and the Triune God of Grace.* Downers Grove, IL: IVP, 1996.

Townley, Cathy. *Missional Worship: Increasing Attendance and Expanding the Boundaries of your Church.* St. Louis, MO: Chalice, 2011.

Ursinus, Zacharias. *Commentary on the Heidelberg Catechism.* Grand Rapids: Eerdmans, 1954.

VanGelder, Craig, and Dwight Zscheile. *The Missional Church in Perspective: Mapping Trends and Shaping the Conversation.* Grand Rapids: Baker Academic, 2011.

Westermann, Claus. *Praise and Lament in the Psalms.* Translated by Keith R. Crim and Richard N. Soulen. Atlanta: John Knox, 1981.

Witvliet, John D. *Worship Seeking Understanding: Windows into Christian Practice.* Grand Rapids: Baker Academic, 2003.

Woltersdorff, Nicholas. "Liturgy and Lament." *Perspectives* (June/July 2012). Accessed February 2, 2017. https://perspectivesjournal.org/blog/2012/06/01/liturgy-and-lament/.

The Worship Sourcebook. 2nd ed. Grand Rapids: Calvin Institute of Christian Worship, 2013.

Wright, Christopher J. H. *The Mission of God: Unlocking the Bible's Grand Narrative.* Downers Grove, IL: IVP Academic, 2006.

———. *The Mission of God's People: A Biblical Theology of the Church's Mission.* Grand Rapids: Zondervan, 2010.

Name/Subject Index

anointing, 14, 36–43, 51, 100
Apostles' Creed, 55, 57, 80
art(s), 57–58, 87, 93–94
attraction, 3, 83–85, 91–93
audience, worshipers as an, 6

baptism, 49 *see* Jesus *and* worship, elements of
Barrett, Lois, 66
Belgic Confession, 50
Berkhof, Louis, 100
Bible, 1, 8, 33–35, 85, 101,
Billings, J. Todd, 13–14
body, human, 7–8, 78–79, 80–81, 85–87, 93–94, 96
body of Christ, 11, 14, 24, 89
Bavinck, Herman, 38n4
Bruner, Frederick Dale, 38

calendar, liturgical, 2, 17–18
    Advent, 2, 17–18, 48, 81, 112–13, 118, 122–23, 124–31
    Ascension Day, 18, 96, 99, 107–11
    Ash Wednesday, 54, 62
    Baptism of Jesus, 18
    Christmas, 2, 9, 18, 20–32, 33–35, 126
    Easter, 18, 21, 48, 74–75, 77, 80, 87–94, 118
    Epiphany, 18, 34–51
    Good Friday, 18, 54, 58, 74, 77
    Lent, 18, 34, 53–73, 133
    Palm Sunday, 48, 58
    Pentecost, 18, 96, 99–100, 106–11

    Trinity Sunday, 18
Calvin, John, 23–24, 31, 40, 55, 76
Canons of Dort, 89
Chan, Simon, 2, 5
church
    building, 3, 27, 57–58, 110 *see* art(s) *and* décor
    denomination, 113–14, 123
    growth, 3
community, 11–12,
confidence, 41, 44, 51, 54, 62–63, 71–73, 82, 95–111, 116, 118
contextualization, 4, 24–25, 27–28, 92–93
Cosper, Mike, 9, 69, 71–72, 107, 130
creation, 9, 40, 62, 67, 81–82, 85–87, 93, 101, 112, 123–24
Crump, David, 98
culture, 24–26, 28, 29, 87, 88, 93–94, 105, 118–22, 123, 125

death, 44, 54, 61–63, 67, 76, 78, 86, 91
décor, 57–58, 93, 110
deliverance, 74–82, 84, 92
DeYoung, Kevin, 45–46
disciples of Jesus, 1, 35, 36, 38, 43, 45, 46, 53, 59, 133
doubt, 75–80

election, 8
embodied, 7–8
eternal life, 62, 67, 80
evangelism, 1, 20, 43–44, 45–47, 48, 95, 105, 118

Name/Subject Index

evil, 41, 44, 46, 53, 61–62, 67, 71, 81, 83, 101, 112–21, 127
Exodus, the, 75–80, 84

faith, 38, 40, 76–77, 82–83, 95, 97–98, 115, 117
faithfulness, 70
fall, the, 9, 53, 101
family, 29, 117
following Jesus, 52–53
foreigner(s)/immigrant(s)/stranger(s), 74, 84, 113, 114, 127
forgiveness, 27, 35–36, 40–41, 44, 48–49, 56–57, 60, 62, 64–65, 67, 69, 72, 77, 82–83, 85, 88–90, 97–98, 128–29, 133
Frost, Michael, 45, 65, 66, 83

gathering for worship, 11–12, 126
generosity, 27, 29–32, 44, 59, 98
gift(s), 20–21, 26–27, 30
Gilbert, Greg, 45–46
God
    concern for the poor, 22, 84
    Creator, 10, 85
    faithfulness, 22
    forgiveness, 10, 40, 98
    glory, 16, 40, 91–92, 130
    love, 44, 124
    power, 99–102
    presence, 22
    Trinity, 15, 109
gospel, 3, 4, 9, 10, 21, 24–25, 28–30, 43, 45–47, 49, 50, 98, 123, 128
gratitude, 30, 59–60, 63, 65–66, 70, 72
Gross, Bobby, 93
gun control, 88

habit(s), 7–16, 28–29, 35–36, 41–51, 68–73, 106–11, 116–18, 124
heaven, 18, 37, 95–97, 99, 100, 103, 104, 107, 110, 111, 126–27
Heidelberg Catechism, 14, 39–40, 42, 61, 76
Hobbs, Walter C., 105–6

Holy Spirit, 5, 7, 37, 50, 60, 65, 97, 99–111, 120, 134
homelessness, 29, 95
hope, 10, 38, 66–68, 72, 81, 86–87, 122–31, 132–33
hospitality, 25, 27, 32
House, Renee S., 42
humility, 8, 23–27, 44, 58, 64, 69, 82–83, 88, 90
Hunsberger, George R., 92, 125

identity, 113–15, 119–20
imagination, 8–10
Immink, Gerrit, 15
incarnational mission, 24–26, 32
institution(s), 11

Jesus
    ascension, 34, 96–111
    baptism, 34, 35, 37–38, 49, 118
    chief worshiper, 15
    crucifixion, 55–60, 65–66, 70
    death, 52–54, 60–62, 66–68, 70–73
    descent into hell, 60–61
    humility, 23–27, 30, 32, 58
    incarnation, 21–32, 53
    innocence, 55–57, 64–65, 68–70
    intercessor, 97–100, 109
    king, 36–51, 113–18
    Messiah/Christ/anointed, 36–51, 100
    miracle worker, 35–36, 48
    perfect work, 43–45, 49
    peripatetic/earthly ministry, 34–51, 118
    priest, 36–51, 97–98
    prophet/teacher, 36–51
    resurrection, 4, 74–94, 118
    return/second coming, 97, 112–31, 133
    suffering, 52–73
    temptation(s), 37
    threefold office, 36–51
    trial, 55–57
    victor, 41, 44

Name/Subject Index

willingness to suffer, 2, 57–60, 65–66, 70
Judas, 58–59
justification, 76–77, 82–83

kingdom, 34, 44, 52, 54, 102, 112–31
kingly work, 41, 42
Keller, Timothy, 104–5, 119–21
Kreider, Alan and Eleanor, 107
Kuyper, Abraham 38n4

Labberton, Mark, 72, 91
Lewis, C. S., 52
love, 25, 27, 32, 36, 38, 44, 46, 47, 83, 95, 124

Magi, 26–27
marvelous exchange, 21, 23–24, 27–32
metaphor, 8, 10, 94
Meyers, Ruth, 4, 5, 16, 90, 107
mission, broad engagement in, 42–51
missional church(es), 3–4, 24
Möbius Strip, 5, 16
Murray, John, 79
music, 3, 8, 20, 92, 94, 119, 125–26

neighbor(s), 20–21, 24–28, 46, 49, 65, 69, 83, 86–87, 88, 92–93, 95, 103, 126
new creation, 19, 27, 38n4, 62, 67, 85–87, 93, 101, 121, 123–24

Passover, 74, 76, 80, 110
pastor, 9–10, 68, 86
pietism, 66
Pontius Pilate, 55–57
poverty, 84, 117
prayer, 41, 44, 97–111 see worship, elements of
pride, 71
priesthood, 40, 42
prophecy, 40, 42–44

racism, 127, 129
reconciliation, see forgiveness
redemption, 72, 84, 101

Reformation, 17, 42, 60
resurrection of the body, 80–81, 85–87, 93–94
retirement, 101
righteousness, 16, 27, 31, 69, 76–77, 82–83, 88–90, 98, 100, 130
risk, 66–67

sacrifice, 15, 23, 37, 40, 44, 66, 78, 81, 90, 97–98, 133
sanctification, 78–79, 83–85 91–93, 119, 122
Schmit, Clayton, 8
school, 101, 106, 119
Schoon, Christopher J., 2
sexuality, 88
shame, 29, 75, 82
Sherman, Robert P., 27, 37–38
Smedes, Lewis, 13, 113
Smith, James K. A., 7, 10, 106, 127
spiritual gift(s), 97, 105, 119–20
Stark, Rodney, 122
Stookey, Laurence Hull, 64, 74
story(-ies), 8–11, 33–35, 56, 101, 107, 119–31
Stutzman, Linford L., 92, 125
suffering, 1, 22, 75, 103, 108, 120, 128

temptation, 41, 78, 97, 119
Thanksgiving Day, 9
Torrance, James B., 15
tradition(s), 11, 27

Ursinus, Zacharias, 42

Van Gelder, Craig, 64
volunteering, 4, 95

Westminster catechism, 3
Witvliet, John D., 28, 125
Wise Men, see Magi
Woltersdorff, Nicholas, 103
Word, the, see Bible
work/job/career, 101, 105–6, 109, 111, 119
worship
  as a means to an end, 2–6

Name/Subject Index

    as a product to be consumed, 6
    attractional, 3
    on Sunday, 124–25
    participation in, 6–12
    private and personal, 15
worship, elements of, 17
    Advent candle, 127
    baptism, 20, 49, 72
    benediction, *see* sending
    call to worship, 8, 47–48, 72, 107, 126–27
    charge, *see* sending
    commissioning, 12, 31, 131
    confession, 8, 10, 48, 68, 71–72, 90
    lament, 71–72, 103, 128–29
    Lord's Supper, 8, 10, 29, 31, 50, 70, 89–90, 94, 110–11, 129–30
    mutual greeting, 90
    offering, 29–30, 70
    passing the peace, 4, 90
    praise and adoration, 10, 72, 91–92, 107
    prayer for illumination, 49–50
    prayers, 50, 72, 88–89, 93, 107–9
    sending 29, 51, 109, 130
    sermon, 1–2, 8, 9, 10, 49–50
worship wars, 3
Wright, Christopher, 46, 61–62, 66–67, 85–86, 91, 101, 103, 117, 121–22

Zscheile, Dwight, 64

Scripture Index

OLD TESTAMENT

Genesis
2:15	86
9:10	81
12:1	114
15:6	76

Exodus
2:23	78
4:22	78
5:1–5	78
5:21	80
10:21–29	78
12:12–13	80
12:31–32	80
12:36	80
22:21	114
23:9	84, 114
28	37

Leviticus
19:34	114
25:38	84
25:42	84
25:55	84

Deuteronomy
10:19	114
15:12	84
15:15	84
24:18	84
31	100

1 Samuel
10	37

2 Kings
2	100
2:15	100

2 Chronicles
28–29	100

Psalm
2	37
24:1	117
29:3	48
96	91–92
104–6	107
104:30	107
110	37
131	71

Isaiah
11:3–9	129
61	37
65	81, 121

Scripture Index

Zechariah

9:9	58

NEW TESTAMENT

Matthew

4	38
4:4	38
4:6	38
4:9	38
4:17	38
4:19	38
4:24	38
5:21–30	69
6:1	82
6:1–18	71
6:14–15	49
7:23	115
7:29	49
11:28–30	47–48
16:24–25	65
17:20	98
18:21–35	84
19:14	48
21:4–5	58
21:22	98
25:41	115
26:46	1
28:20	96, 102

Mark

1:11	37
1:17–18	43
1:21–28	48, 49
1:29–31	48
2:7	35
4:35–41	48
9:5	36
9:29	98
11:24	98
14:50	53
14:54	53

Luke

4:18	37
5:27–29	25
6:36	84
10	25
11:5–8	98
17:6	98
18:1–8	98
19:1–5	25
21:34	128
22:16	130
22:18	130
22:42	59
23:49	53
24:52–53	100

John

1:1–5	22
1:5	25
1:10–11	25
1:14	22
4:24	11
6:26–27	130
7:1–5	35
8	49
12:23–26	52
13:27	58
13:29	59
14–16	22
14:2–3	97
14:13	98
14:18	96
15:4	79
15:7	98
15:16	50
16:7	99
16:23	50, 98
18:38	55
19:4	55
19:6	55
19:16	56
19:30	77
20:14–16	110
20:21–22	102
20:22	134
20:23	133

Scripture Index

Acts

1:8	99, 102
1:9	96
2:24	78
2:42–45	11
5:31	98
10	84
11:26	13

Romans

3:10	116
3:21	62
3:23	116
4:25	77
6:1–2	60
6:1–11	66
6:4	60
6:5	16, 78
6:6	71, 78
6:18	60, 78
7:24	78
8:1–17	60
8:11	79
12	11
12:1	66, 78
15:13	109

1 Corinthians

10–13	11
11:20	89
15	81
15:22–26	118

2 Corinthians

1:11	103
5:19–21	64–65
5:21	23
8:9	30
13:14	109

Galatians

4:4	23
5:16	16
5:22–23	93

Ephesians

2:6	96
2:9	82
2:14–16	62
4:7–8	97
4:7–16	102
4:12–13	16
4:15–16	15
4:32	84
6	103
6:9	84

Philippians

1:20–26	67
2	25
2:6–8	23

Colossians

1:15–16	117
1:15–20	81
1:20	62
2:14	62
2:15	72
3:13	84

1 Thessalonians

4:17–18	68
5:5	114

1 Timothy

2:1	102
2:1–6	88–89

Hebrews

4:14	98
6:19	98
8:4	98
9:14	98
10:14	40
10:18	40
11:9–10	114
11:13	114

Scripture Index

1 Peter

2:5	40
2:11	114

2 Peter

3	81, 121

1 John

1:9	56
3:16–17	84

Revelation

1:13–16	87
3:5	115
4	87
5:9	127
20:12	116
21	121
21:5	112

www.ingramcontent.com/pod-product-compliance
Lightning Source LLC
Chambersburg PA
CBHW022126160426
43197CB00009B/1166